Simon Gray

QUARTERMAINE'S TERMS

EYRE METHUEN · LONDON

Quartermaine's Terms was first published in 1981 by Eyre
   Methuen Ltd.,
11 New Fetter Lane, London EC4P 4EE
Copyright © 1981 by Simon Gray
Set in IBM 10pt. Journal by 𝄃\Tek-Art, Croydon, Surrey
Printed and bound in Great Britain by Fakenham Press Ltd,
Fakenham, Norfolk

ISBN 0 413 49140 4

CAUTION
All rights in this play are strictly reserved and application for
performance etc should be made before rehearsal to Judy Daish
Associates, 122 Wigmore Street, London W1H 9FE. No
performance may be given unless a licence has been obtained.

QUARTERMAINE'S TERMS

Set in the 1960s in a school teaching English to foreigners, Simon Gray's new play follows the varying fortunes of the school and its staff — particularly of St. John Quartermaine, whose naive responses to the emotional crises going on all round him makes him as rich a comic creation as Gray's earlier protagonists, Butley and Simon Hench in *Otherwise Engaged*.

The premiere production of *Quartermaine's Terms* is scheduled for July 1981 with Harold Pinter directing and Edward Fox in the lead.

The photograph of Simon Gray on the back cover is reproduced by courtesy of the Sunday Telegraph.

For BERYL

Quartermaine's Terms was first presented by Michael Codron at the Queen's Theatre, London, on 28 July 1981, with the following cast:

ST. JOHN QUARTERMAINE	Edward Fox
ANITA MANCHIP	Jenny Quayle
MARK SACKLING	Peter Birch
EDDIE LOOMIS	Robin Bailey
DEREK MEADLE	Glyn Grain
HENRY WINDSCAPE	James Grout
MELANIE GARTH	Prunella Scales

Directed by Harold Pinter
Designed by Eileen Diss
Lighting by Leonard Tucker

The Set: The staff-room of the Cull-Loomis School of English for foreigners, Cambridge, or rather a section of the staff-room — the last quarter of it. On stage are French windows, a long table, lockers for members of the staff, pegs for coats etc, and a number of armchairs; on the table a telephone, newspapers and magazines. This is the basic set, to which, between scenes and between the two Acts, additions can be made to suggest the varying fortunes of the school. Off stage, left, a suggestion of hard-backed chairs, and off left, a door to the main corridor of the school, where the class-rooms are.

The period: early 1960s.

ACT ONE

Scene One

Monday morning, spring term. The French windows are open. It is about 9.30. Sunny.

QUARTERMAINE is sitting with his feet up, hands folded on his lap, staring ahead. From off, outside the French windows, in the garden, the sound of foreign voices excited, talking, laughing etc; passing by. As these recede:

ANITA comes through the French windows carrying a briefcase.

ANITA. 'Morning, St. John.

QUARTERMAINE. Oh hello Anita, but I say, you know — (*Getting up.*) you look — you look different, don't you?

ANITA. Do I? Oh — my hair probably. I've put it up.

QUARTERMAINE. Well, it looks — looks really terrific! Of course I liked it the other way too, tumbling down your shoulders.

ANITA. It hasn't tumbled down my shoulders for three years, St. John.

QUARTERMAINE. Oh. How was it then before you changed it?

ANITA. Back in a pony tail. (*She indicates.*)

QUARTERMAINE. That's it. Yes. Well, I liked it like that, too.

ANITA. Thank you. Oh by the way, Nigel asked me to apologise again for having to cancel dinner. He was afraid he was a little abrupt on the 'phone.

QUARTERMAINE. Oh Lord no, not at all — besides, it's lucky he *was* abrupt, you know how Mrs Harris hates me using the 'phone, she stands right beside me glowering, but I managed to understand exactly what he was getting at, something to do with — with a lecture he had to prepare, wasn't it.

ANITA. No, it was the new magazine they're starting. The first issue's coming out shortly and they still haven't got enough material so they had to call a panic editorial meeting — it went on until three in the morning —

QUARTERMAINE. Oh. Poor old Nigel. But it sounds tremendously — tremendously exciting —

ANITA. Oh yes. Well, they're all very excited about it, anyway, they're determined it shouldn't just be another little Cambridge literary magazine, you know, but they want to preserve the Cambridge style and tone. Anyway, I'm sorry we couldn't have the dinner, and at such short notice. Did you find anything else to do?

QUARTERMAINE. Oh yes, yes, I was fine, don't worry, tell Nigel, because just after he 'phoned, old Henry 'phoned, to invite me around.

ANITA. What luck. For dinner?

QUARTERMAINE. No, to baby-sit, actually.

ANITA. To baby-sit. But their oldest — Susan isn't it? — must be nearly fourteen.

QUARTERMAINE. Yes, but apparently she's working away for her 'O' levels — she's very bright — taking it years in advance and all that, so they wanted her not to have to worry about the young ones, you see — in fact, they really hadn't meant to go out, and then they discovered that there was some film they wanted to see at The Arts, some old German classic they seem to be very fond of, about — about a child-murderer as far as I could make out from what Henry told me. So that was all right.

ANITA. You enjoyed it, then?

QUARTERMAINE. Oh Lord yes, well children you know are such — such — it took me a bit of time to get them used to me, of course, as the smallest one, the one they call little Fanny — very charming, very charming — cried when she saw me — she hates it when Henry and Fanny go out, you see — and then the boy — my word, what a little devil, full of mischief, told me little Fanny had drowned in the bath and when I ran in there she was — lying face down — hair floating around — and I stood there thinking, you know, (*He laughs.*) Lord, what am I going to say to Henry and Fanny particularly when they get back, especially after seeing a film like that — but it turned out it was only an enormous Raggidy Anne doll, and little Fanny was hiding under her bed — because Ben had told her I was going to eat her up — (*He laughs.*) but I got them settled down in the end, in fact it would have been sooner if Susan hadn't kept coming out of her room to scream at them for interrupting her studying — and anyway Henry and Fanny came back quite early. In about an hour, as a matter of fact.

ANITA. Well, at least you had a bit of an evening with them then.

QUARTERMAINE. Oh rather — except that Fanny had a terrible headache from straining to read the subtitles, that's why they'd had to leave, a very poor print apparently — then Henry got involved in a — an argument with Ben, who'd got up when he heard them come in so I felt, you know, they rather wanted me out of the way —

The sound of the door opening, during the above. Footsteps.

Oh hello Mark, top of the morning to you, have a good weekend?

SACKLING *appears on stage. He is carrying a briefcase, is unshaven, looks ghastly.*

ANITA (*looking at him in concern*). Are you all right?

SACKLING. Yes, yes, fine, fine. (*He drops the briefcase, slumps into a chair.*)

ANITA. Are you growing a beard?

SACKLING. What? Oh Christ! (*Feeling his chin.*) I forgot!

ANITA. But there must be several days' stubble there.

SACKLING. Haven't been to bed you see. All weekend.

QUARTERMAINE. Ah, been hard at it, eh?

SACKLING. What?

QUARTERMAINE. Hard at it. The old writing.

SACKLING *grunts.*

Terrific!

ANITA. Oh, I've got a message from Nigel, by the way, he asked me to ask you to hurry up with an extract, they're desperate to get it into the first issue, he says don't worry about whether it's self-contained, they can always shove it in as 'Work in Progress' or something.

SACKLING. Right.

ANITA. You look to me as if you've over-done it — are you sure you're all right?

QUARTERMAINE. I say, how's old Camelia?

SACKLING. (*barks out a laugh*). Oh fine! Just — fine!

QUARTERMAINE. Terrific, and little Tom too?

SACKLING. Tom too, oh yes, Tom too.

QUARTERMAINE. The last time I saw him he was teething, standing there in his high chair dribbling away like anything, while Camelia was sitting on old Mark's lap making faces at him with orange peel in her mouth —

SACKLING *bursts into tears.* ANITA *goes to* SACKLING, *puts her hand on his shoulder.*

QUARTERMAINE. What? Oh — oh Lord!

SACKLING. Sorry — sorry — I'll be all right — still — still digesting.

QUARTERMAINE. Something you had for breakfast, is it? Not kidneys — they can give you terrible heart-burn — especially with mushrooms —

ANITA *shakes her head at him.*

Mmmm?

ANITA. Do you want to talk about it?

SACKLING. I don't want anyone — anyone else to know —

especially not Thomas or Eddie — don't want them dripping their — their filthy compassion all over me.

QUARTERMAINE. What?

ANITA. We're to keep it to ourselves, St. John.

QUARTERMAINE. Oh Lord yes. Of course. What though?

SACKLING. She's left me.

QUARTERMAINE. Who?

ANITA. Camelia, of course.

QUARTERMAINE. What! Old Camelia! On no!

SACKLING. Taking Tom — taking Tom with her.

QUARTERMAINE. Oh, not little Tom too!

SACKLING. Tom too.

ANITA. Well, did she — say why?

SACKLING (*makes an effort, pulls himself together*). She — she — (*He takes an envelope out of his pocket.*) I was upstairs in the attic — writing away — as far as I knew she was downstairs where she usually is — in the kitchen or — ironing — with the television on. And Tom in bed, of course. So I wrote on and on — I felt inspired, quite inspired, a passage about — about what I'd felt when I saw Tom coming out of her womb — so shiny and whole and beautiful — a wonderful passage — full of — full of my love for her and him — and when I finished I went downstairs to her — to read it to her — as I always do when it's something I'm burning with — and she wasn't there — the house was very still, empty, but I didn't think — never occurred to me — so I went up the stairs and into our bedroom and — all her clothes — the suitcases everything — gone — and this — this on the pillow. (*He hands the note to* QUARTERMAINE.)

QUARTERMAINE *takes it, opens it, makes to read it. Stops. Shakes his head.*

ANITA *makes a small move to take it from him.*

QUARTERMAINE (*not noticing*). No, we can't — can we, Anita — really — I mean it's from her to you so — so — (*He hands it back.*)

SACKLING (*takes it back*). 'I'm sorry darling, so sorry oh my darling, but it seems after all that I wasn't cut out to be a writer's wife. I can't stand the strain of it, the lonely evenings, your remoteness, and most of all the feeling that your novel means more to you than Tom and I do. Perhaps that's what being an artist is. Not caring about those who love you. I'm going back to mother's, I'll take the car' — yes, taken the car — she'd take that all right, wouldn't she! — 'as you don't drive, and begin proceedings as soon as I've got a lawyer. Take care, my love, look after yourself, I wish you such success and I know that one day I'll be proud to have been your first wife, just as Tom will be proud to be your father.'

There is a pause.

QUARTERMAINE. Um, son, surely.

SACKLING. What?

QUARTERMAINE. Um, Tom's your son. Not your father. You read out that he was your father. Not your son.

SACKLING. Oh, if only I'd been able to read her that passage — she would have understood my feelings, she'd have known — but what do I do, I can't give up now, not when I'm so close to finishing — my fourth draft — my penultimate draft — I *know* it's the penultimate — then one final one — and — and — so what do I do — I can't think — can't think —

LOOMIS *enters through the French windows. He walks awkwardly, has thick glasses, is carrying a file.*

LOOMIS. Good morning, good morning, Anita my dear, Mark. I trust you all had a good weekend?

QUARTERMAINE. ⎫
ANITA.   ⎬ Yes, thank you Eddie.
SACKLING.   ⎭

LOOMIS. I'm just on my way through to do my little welcome speech, with a small dilation this time on the problems of our Cambridge landladies, we've just heard that our faithful Mrs Cornley is refusing to take any of our students except what she calls traditional foreigners, all over some dreadful

misunderstanding she's had with those three really delightful
Turks we sent her, over the proper function of the bathroom
— such a nuisance, Thomas has been on the 'phone to her for
hours — but still, I suppose the problems of a flourishing
school — nine Japanese have turned up, by the way, instead
of the anticipated six, and as it was three last time we can
hope for a round dozen next — Mark, is it these fast-fading
old eyes of mine, or did you forget to shave this morning,
and yesterday morning, even?

SACKLING. No, no — I'm thinking of growing a beard, Eddie.

LOOMIS. Alas! And what saith the fair Camelia to that?

SACKLING (*mutters*). I don't think she'll mind.

LOOMIS. Mmmm?

SACKLING. I don't — I don't think she'll mind, Eddie.

LOOMIS. Good, good — Anita, my dear, may I pay you a
compliment?

ANITA. Yes please, Eddie.

LOOMIS. I like your hair even more that way.

ANITA. Well, thank you Eddie, actually I put it up for a dinner
party we had last night — and thought I'd give it a longer run
— it was a sort of editorial dinner, you see — (*Realizing.*)

LOOMIS. Ah! And the magazine's progressing well, or so we
gathered from Nigel. We bumped into him on the Backs, on
Saturday afternoon, did he tell you?

ANITA. No. No he didn't.

LOOMIS. He was having a conference with one of his
co-editors, I suppose it was.

ANITA. Oh. Thomas Pine.

LOOMIS. No no, I don't think Thomas Pine, my dear, but
co-editress I should have said, shouldn't I, one can't be too
precise these days.

ANITA. Oh. Was she — blonde and — rather pretty.

LOOMIS. Oh, very pretty — at least Thomas was much smitten,

you know what an eye he's got.

ANITA. Ah, then that would be Amanda Southgate, yes, I expect he was trying to persuade her to take on all the dog-bodying — you know, hounding contributors, keeping the printers at bay — she's terrifically efficient. She's an old friend of mine. I used to go to school with her sister. (*A little pause*.) She's smashing, actually.

LOOMIS. Good good — now St. John, what was it Thomas asked me to tell you — or was it Henry and Melanie I'm to tell what to? Oh yes, this of course. (*He hands him a post-card from the file*.) We couldn't resist having a look, post-cards being somehow in the public domain, one always thinks. At least when they're other people's (*He laughs*.) Do read it out to Mark and Anita, don't be modest St. John.

QUARTERMAINE. Um, I must writing to thanking you for all excellent times in your most heppy clesses, your true Ferdinand Boller. Lord! (*He laughs*.)

LOOMIS. And which one was he, can you recall?

QUARTERMAINE. Oh. Well, you know a — a German —

LOOMIS. Post-marked Zurich, I believe, so more likely a Swiss.

QUARTERMAINE. Oh yes, that's right, a Swiss, a — a well, rather large, Eddie, with his hair cut en brosse and — round face — in his forties or so, and —

LOOMIS. — and wearing lederhosen, perhaps, and good at yodelling, no no, St. John, I don't think I quite believe in your rather caricature Swiss, I suspect you must have made rather more of an impression on Herr Ferdinand Boller than he managed to make on you, still I suppose that's better than the other way around, and his sentiments are certainly quite a tribute — would that his English were, too, eh? But do try to remember them St. John, match names to faces. (*He laughs*.) And on that subject, you haven't forgotten Mr Middleton begins this morning, have you?

QUARTERMAINE. Who, Eddie?

LOOMIS. Middleton. Dennis Middleton, St. John, Henry told

you all about him at the last staff meeting, he wrote to us from Hull expressing such an intelligent interest in the techniques of teaching English as a foreign language that Thomas invited him for an interview, and was so taken by the genuineness of his manner that he offered him some teaching — only part-time to begin with, of course, until we see how things go — anyway, he should be here any minute, so whilst I'm making the students welcome perhaps you would be doing the same for him, and tell him that either Thomas or I will be along before the bell to introduce him to his first class, which is, I believe Intermediary Dictation — Mark?

SACKLING. Mmm?

LOOMIS. Middleton, Mark.

SACKLING (*blankly*). Yes. Yes. Right Eddie.

LOOMIS. See you all at the bell then — (*He walks off, stage left. Then sound of him stopping. A slight pause.*) Oh Mark, there is one other thing — if I could just have a quick private word —

SACKLING. What? Oh — oh yes — (*He gets up. As he goes over:*)

LOOMIS (*takes a few necessary steps to be on stage. In a lowered voice*). Nothing important, Mark, merely Thomas wanted me to mention, in a by-the-way spirit, one of our French students Mlle Jeanette LeClerc, do you recall her?

SACKLING. Oh. Yes. I think so. Yes.

LOOMIS. She's written complaining that you forgot to return two or three pieces of her work, an essay and two comprehension passages I believe she listed, as I say, not cataclysmic in itself, but as Thomas always points out, so much of our reputation depends on Jeanette passing on to Lucien what Lucien then passes to Gabrielle, so do make a note of which students are leaving when and make sure of getting every item back before they go. Mark?

SACKLING *tautly nods.*

Good, good, and may I put in my personal plea against the beard, I do think they make even the handsomest chaps

red-eyed and snivelly looking, I don't want to end up begging
Camelia to be Delilah to your Samson, eh, and think of poor
little Tom too, having to endure Daddy's whiskers against his
chubby young cheeks at cuddle-time —

SACKLING *rushes past him out of the door.*

But — but — what did I say? A little professional criticism —
it *can't* have been about the beard, I couldn't have been more
playful.

QUARTERMAINE. Oh, it's not your fault, Eddie, is it Anita,
you see the poor chap's had a — a horrible weekend —

ANITA (*warningly, cutting in*). Yes, up all night, working at his
novel. I'll go and see if he's all right. (*She goes off, left.*)

LOOMIS. I see. Well that's all very well, after all nobody could
respect Mark's literary ambitions more than Thomas and
myself, but we really can't have him running about in this
sort of state, what on earth would the students make of it if
he were to gallop emotionally off in the middle of a
dictation —

MEADLE *appears at the French windows.*

MEADLE. Um, is this the staff room, please?

*He is hot and flustered, wearing bicycle clips, carrying a
brief-case, and mopping his brow.*

LOOMIS. Yes, what do you want — oh, of course, it's
Mr Middleton, isn't it? Our new member of staff.

MEADLE. Well, yes — well, Meadle, actually, Derek Meadle.

LOOMIS. Yes, yes, Derek Meadle, well, I'm Eddie Loomis, the
Principal. One of two Principals, as you know, as you've met
Mr Cull of course, and this is St. John Quartermaine who's
been with us since our school started, and you've come down
to join us from Sheffield, isn't it.

MEADLE. Yes sir, well Hull actually.

LOOMIS. Hull, good good — and when did you arrive?

MEADLE. Yesterday afternoon.

LOOMIS. And found yourself a room?

MEADLE. Yes, yes thank you, sir.

LOOMIS. Good good, and found yourself a bicycle too, I see.

MEADLE (*who throughout all this has been standing rather awkwardly, keeping face-on to* LOOMIS.) Yes, sir. My landlady — I happened to ask her where could be a good place to buy a second-hand one, not being familiar with the shops, and she happened to mention that her son had left one behind in the basement and I could have it for two pounds so I —

LOOMIS (*interrupting*). Good good, most enterprising — at least of your landlady. (*He laughs.*) But Mr Meadle I've got to have a little talk with the students, and Mr Cull is still looking after enrolment, but one of us will be back at the bell to introduce you to your first class — intermediary comprehension itsn't it —

MEADLE. Dictation sir.

LOOMIS. So I'll leave you in St. John's capable hands —

MEADLE. Yes sir. Thank you.

LOOMIS. Oh, one thing, though, Mr Meadle — sir us no sirs, we're very informal here — I'm Eddie, Mr Cull is Thomas, and you're Dennis.

MEADLE. Oh, well thank you very much —

LOOMIS (*as the sound of students' voices is heard off, crossing the garden*). Ah, and here they are — (*He goes off, left.*)

QUARTERMAINE. Well, I must say — jolly glad to have you with us — I think you'll enjoy it here — the staff is — well, they're terrific — and the students are — well, they're very interesting, coming from all quarters of the globe, so to speak — but look, why don't you come in properly and sit down and — and make yourself at home.

MEADLE. Yes, thanks, but — well, you see, the trouble is I've had an accident.

QUARTERMAINE. Really? Oh Lord!

MEADLE. Yes, I didn't want to go into it in front of Mr Loomis,
— Eddie — not quite the way to start off one's first day in a
new job — but — well — here — you'd better see for yourself.

He turns. His trousers are rent at the seat.

How bad is it, actually?

QUARTERMAINE. Well — they're — they're — a bit of a write-
off, I'm afraid. How did it happen?

MEADLE. Oh, usual combination of unexpected circumstances,
eh? (*He laughs.*) For one thing the bicycle — I suspected there
might be something wrong with it for two pounds, but I
checked everything — the brakes, the mudguards, the wheels,
the inner tubes, even the pump and the dynamo. The only
thing I didn't examine meticulously was the seat. There was
the minutest bit of spring sticking up, and I suppose it
worked its way into my trousers as I was pedalling here. The
worm in the apple, eh? (*He laughs.*) But even so I'd probably
have been all right if it hadn't been for a little pack of
Japanese coming up the school drive. They were laughing and
chattering so much among themselves — not the usual idea of
Japanese at all — You know, formal and keeping a distance
from each other — (*He laughs.*) didn't hear my bell until I was
almost on top of them, and then a big chap with a bald head
— I didn't realise they came in that sort of size either —
stepped right out in front of me — I was going pretty
quickly, I have to admit — wanted to be in good time, you
see for my first day — and of course I lost control on the
gravel and skidded and had to leap sideways off the bike. But
with my trousers snagged I only half-made it. They were very
tactful about it, by the way. Averted their eyes to show they
hadn't seen it, and went on into the office. What they call
saving face, I believe. My face, in this case. Oh, except for
the big bald one. I had the impression he found it rather
amusing — but of course the question is what do I do about
it? I mean I don't really want to spend my first day going
about like this, do I? People might get the impression it's
my normal attire. (*He laughs. But this speech should be
delivered to convey a simmering rage and desperation*

behind the attempt at an insouciant manner, and of a natural
North Country accent held in check under stress.)

QUARTERMAINE. Well, you know old chap, I think the best
thing would be to go back and change. Don't worry about
being late — I'll explain what happened —

MEADLE. Ah, yes, but into what is the question.

QUARTERMAINE. Well — into another pair of trousers, I —
I suppose.   -

MEADLE. Yes, but you see, I haven't got another pair is the
problem. An elderly gentleman on the train yesterday spilt
his chocolate out of his thermos right over the pair I
happened to have on, so the first thing I did when I got in —
irony of ironics — was to take them to the cleaners. And my
trunk, which I'd sent on from Hull and which contained my
suit and my other two pairs, hasn't arrived yet. So there it is.
Hot chocolate, a broken spring, a pack of unusually
gregarious Japanese and British Rail, all working together in
complete harmony to bring me to my first day of my new
job looking like Oliver and Hardy. What do I do? Any
suggestions? I mean if I pull them really high — like this —
(*Pulling them up.*) and leave my clips on — does it still show?

QUARTERMAINE. Well, just a little — well, not really — well,
I say, I'll tell you what — if you can get your jacket down
just a fraction —

MEADLE (*he pulls it down*). — but if I keep my hands in —
(*Putting them in the pockets, and pushing down.*) what
about it?

QUARTERMAINE. How does it feel?

MEADLE (*laughs*). Well — unnatural. Extremely unnatural.
(*Taking a few steps.*)

QUARTERMAINE. Actually, you look rather — rather
formidable actually.

MEADLE (*taking another step or so*). No no — (*Exploding into
a violent rage.*) Bloody hell, I'm meant to be teaching, I can't
go round like this all day, everybody will think I'm some sort

of buffoon — this is the sheerest — the sheerest —

WINDSCAPE *enters through the French windows. He is carrying a briefcase, wears bicycle clips, smokes a pipe.*

WINDSCAPE. Hello, St. John.

QUARTERMAINE. Oh — oh hello Henry — um, come and meet our new chap — (*To* MEADLE:) Henry's our academic tutor — syllabus and all that —

WINDSCAPE (*comes over*). Oh yes, of course, very glad to have you with us, Merton, isn't it?

QUARTERMAINE. Middleton, actually.

MEADLE. Meadle, as a matter of fact.

QUARTERMAINE. That's right. Sorry. Dennis Meadle.

WINDSCAPE. Well, whatever yours happens to be —

MEADLE. Derek. Derek Meadle.

WINDSCAPE. — mine is Windscape. Henry Windscape. How do you do?

MEADLE (*he gets his hand out of his pocket, they shake hands,* MEADLE *replaces his hand*). How do you do?

QUARTERMAINE. I say, how were they in the end, Susan, little Fanny and old Ben — and Fanny's headache?

WINDSCAPE. Oh fine thank you, St. John, fine — I didn't get Susan to bed until midnight of course (*To* MEADLE:) she's studying for her 'O' levels — a couple of years in advance — and — and Fanny had rather a bad moment when she went into the lavatory because of Raggidy Anne sitting there — and dripping — she thought it was little Fanny, you see — (*Laughing.*)

QUARTERMAINE. Oh Lord, I forgot —

WINDSCAPE. St. John was good enough to come over and sit with our three last night — we went to see 'M' you know — such a fine film — so delicate and human in its treatment of a — a sexual freak and Peter Lorre — unfortunately the print was a trifle worn — but still — memorable — memorable —

but isn't it interesting — on another subject — this English
thing about names, how we forget them the second we hear
them. Just now, for instance, when St. John was introducing
you. Unlike Americans for instance. (*He puffs and pulls on his
pipe throughout this speech.* MEADLE *nods and chuckles
tensely.*) I suppose because we — the English that is — are so
busy looking at the person the name represents — or *not*
looking, being English (*He laughs.*) that we don't take in the
name itself — whereas the Americans, you see, make a
point of beginning with the name — when one's
introduced they repeat it endlessly. 'This is Dennis Meadle.
Dennis Meadle, why hello Dennis, and how long have you
been in this country Dennis, this is Dennis Meadle dear,
Dennis was just telling me how much he liked our fair city,
weren't you Dennis . . .' (*All this in an execrable imitation
of an American accent.*) And — and so forth, and in no time
at all they've learnt what you're called by even if not who
you are (*He laughs.*) while we, the English, being more
empirical, don't learn your name until you yourself have
taken on a complicated reality — you and your name grow,
so to speak, in associated stages in our memories, until what
you are as Dennis Meadle and the sounds Dennis Meadle are
inseparable which is actually — when you think about it —
a radical division in ways of perceiving that goes back to the
Middle Ages in the Nominalists — the name callers — calling
the name preceeding the object, so to speak, and the
realists —

During this, MELANIE *has entered through the French
windows. She puts her briefcase on the table.*

— who believed the object preceeded the name — but one
could go on and on; there's Melanie, Melanie come and meet
our new chap —

QUARTERMAINE. Hello Melanie, have a good weekend?

MELANIE. Yes thanks, St. John, you're in top form for a
Monday morning Henry, how do you do, I'm Melanie Garth.

MEADLE. Meadle. Derek Meadle.

MELANIE. And you've come to reinforce us, well we certainly could do with you, Thomas was just telling me about the enrolment chaos, you'll be getting a lot of over-spill from my groups, I can tell you.

WINDSCAPE. Melanie's our Elementary Conversation specialist, by the way.

MELANIE. Oh, I don't know about specialist, Henry. Henry's our only real specialist here, he specializes in — well, everything, doesn't he, St. John, from pronunciation to British Life and Institutions, but what I enjoyed most about the sight of you two philosophising away here was that you both still had your bicycle clips on — as if you'd met on a street corner —

WINDSCAPE (*laughing*). Good heavens, so they are. Thank you for reminding me, my dear, whenever I forget to take them off I spend hours after school hunting for them — (*He bends to take them off.*)

MEADLE *grinning and distraught, makes a gesture towards taking his off.*

QUARTERMAINE (*taking this in*). I say — I say, Melanie, how's — um, how's mother?

MELANIE. Top form, thanks, St. John, her left leg's still giving her bother, and the stairs are a dreadful strain, you know, because of this sudden vertigo, but yesterday she managed to hobble down to the corner-shop all by herself, and was halfway back by the time I came to pick her up.

QUARTERMAINE. Oh, that's terrific! Melanie's mother's just recovering from a thingmebob.

MELANIE. Stroke, if you please, St. John. She insists on the proper term, she hates euphemisms.

WINDSCAPE. Not surprisingly, as Melanie's mother was Cambridge's first lady of philology — the first woman ever to hold the chair in it — I had the honour of being supervised by her in my second year as an undergraduate — and although she's retired she was still very much a behind-the-scenes force on the Faculty until she had her — little upset a few months ago. And will be again, I suspect, as she appears to be coming to terms with her condition in a characteristically — characteristically indomitable —

MEADLE. I have an aunt who had a stroke a year ago. She was the active sort too. Of course not a professor but — very active. In her own way. She went in for jam.

MELANIE. And how is *she* coping?

MEADLE. Well, she was doing splendidly until she had the next. Now she's pretty well out of it altogether, my uncle has to do virtually everything for her. But then that's one of the usual patterns, they said at the hospital. First a mild stroke, followed by a worse stroke, and then, if that doesn't do the job — (*He gestures.*) But in a sense it's worse for my uncle, he's an independent old fellow, used to leading his own life —

MELANIE. Yes, well, Mr Meadle, I'm sorry for your aunt — and for your uncle — but sufficient unto the day, sufficient unto the day — if you'll excuse me, I haven't sorted out my first hour's comprehension — (*She picks up the briefcase, goes to her locker.*)

WINDSCAPE. Of course that's only *one* of the possible patterns — there are many cases of complete — or — or more than merely partial recovery — if I might — might just — Melanie puts on a remarkably brave front, but don't be led astray, she's an intensely feeling person who knows very well the likely outcome of her mother's — her mother's — she's deeply attached to her, as you probably gathered, isn't she, St. John.

QUARTERMAINE. Oh Lord yes!

WINDSCAPE. I hope you don't mind my saying it?

MEADLE. No, no. Thank you. Thank you.

WINDSCAPE. Good man! (*He puts his hand on* MEADLE's *shoulder*). Well, I'd better unpack my own — (*He goes over to his locker, looking towards* MELANIE, *who is standing still by hers.*)

MEADLE (*smiling tightly, and in a low voice*). Don't think I can stand much more of this. Hardly know what I'm saying —

really put my foot in it —

QUARTERMAINE. Well, why don't you just tell them — I mean, it's only a torn pair of bags —

MEADLE. It's too late now, I've left it too late. I can't just clap my hands for attention, oh by the way, everybody, come and look at my trousers, ha ha ha, what I need is safety pins — and then a few minutes in the toilet — can you get me some?

QUARTERMAINE. I'll nip over to the office —

MEADLE. Well, take me to the toilet first.

LOOMIS (*comes through the French windows*). Good morning Melanie, my dear, good morning Henry — good weekend, I trust?

MELANIE.   ⎫
WINDSCAPE. ⎬ Yes thanks, Eddie.

LOOMIS. All well with mother, I trust.

MELANIE. Yes thanks Eddie. Top form.

LOOMIS. Good, good — and Fanny and the children?

WINDSCAPE. Yes, thanks Eddie — all splendid.

LOOMIS. Good good —

As ANITA *and* SACKLING *enter from the right.*

Ah, and here you are, you two, and quite composed again Mark, I trust —

ANITA. Well Eddie, actually I'm not sure that Mark —

SACKLING *feebly gestures silence to* ANITA.

LOOMIS. And Mr Meadle, I don't know which of you have had the chance to meet him yet, but those who haven't can make their separate introductions, in the meanwhile I'll say a welcome on all our behalves, we're delighted to have you with us — I see you've still got your clips on, by the way, perhaps you'd better remove them or you'll create the impression that you're just pedalling through — (*He laughs.*)

MEADLE *bends to take them off.*

— now as we're all here and there are a few minutes before the bell, I'd like to say a few words, if I may. As you've no doubt realised, we have an exceptionally high enrolment for the month, the highest in the school's career, as a matter of fact. (*Little murmurs.*)

QUARTERMAINE. I say, terrific!

LOOMIS. Yes, very gratifying. You all know how hard Thomas has worked for this. Though he'd loathe to hear me say it. But what he wouldn't mind hearing me say is that in his turn he knows how hard you've worked. I think we all have a right to be proud of our growing reputation as one of the best schools of English — not one of the biggest but one of the best — in Cambridge. Which, when it comes down to it, means in the country. Well and good. Well and good. But success will bring — has already begun to bring — its own problems. (*He gestures to* MEADLE.) As Mr Meadle's presence here testifies. But even with Mr Meadle — or Dennis, as I've already told him I intend to call him — with Dennis to help us, there is going to be a considerable strain on our resources. Perhaps a few too many students to a class-room, more work to take home and correct, more difficulties in developing personal contact — that so crucial personal contact — with students many of whom are only here for a short time — well, as I say, you've already become familiar with the problems, the problems, as Thomas remarked 'midst the chaos this morning, of a flourishing school — but please remember, I'm reminding *myself* too when I say this, how important it is if we are to continue to flourish —

SACKLING *faints.*

ANITA *cries out, tries to catch him, half supports him, as* WINDSCAPE *gets to him,* QUARTERMAINE *attempts to.*

WINDSCAPE. There — there old chap — I've got you — out of the way, everyone — while I lower him — (*He does so.*) The thing is to keep his head up.

QUARTERMAINE. Yes, right. (*He makes to go round, as* ANITA *runs over, takes* SACKLING's *head, then sits down, gets his head into her lap.*)

WINDSCAPE. Mark — Mark — can you hear me? (*He slaps his cheeks.*) He's right out. (*He puts his hand on* SACKLING's *heart.*) It's very faint. (*Massaging his heart.*) Somebody better telephone for an ambulance.

QUARTERMAINE. Right! (*He makes to go to the telephone.*)

LOOMIS *goes to the telephone, dials.*

WINDSCAPE. And chafe his wrists — and something to put over him — your coat (*To* MEADLE:) Hurry man!

MEADLE *hesitates, takes off his coat as* QUARTERMAINE *struggles out of his.*

WINDSCAPE. Come around — put it over him — over his chest —

MEADLE *does so, as* QUARTERMAINE *stands, jacket half off.*

There — now — now — now —

LOOMIS *finishes speaking, puts the telephone down, comes over, stands looking anxiously down. The bell rings.*

QUARTERMAINE (*also looking down*). Oh Lord! Oh Lord!

Lights.

Scene Two

Some weeks later. Friday afternoon, a few minutes before 5 p.m. The French windows are open. It's a sunny day.

QUARTERMAINE *is putting books and papers away. He is humming to himself. He closes his locker, does a few elegant dance steps, and then goes into a tap dance, at which he is surprisingly adept.*

LOOMIS *enters through the French windows, watches* QUARTERMAINE.

QUARTERMAINE (*sees* LOOMIS, *stops*). Oh Lord! (*He laughs.*) Hello Eddie.

LOOMIS. You're in sprightly mood, St. John.

QUARTERMAINE. Yes, well Friday evening and off to the theatre and all that — you know.

LOOMIS. And what are you going to see?

QUARTERMAINE. Oh that — that Strindberg, I think it is. At the Arts.

LOOMIS. I believe it's an Ibsen, Hedda Gabler I believe, but tell me — the bell's gone then, has it, I didn't hear it — but then these old ears of mine — (*He laughs.*)

QUARTERMAINE. Ah yes, well I let them out a little early, you see, Eddie.

LOOMIS. Why?

QUARTERMAINE. Well, it was the special Life and Institutions lecture, you see, and I chose Oxford Colleges with slides — to give them the other point of view, for once (*He laughs.*) but of course the old projector broke —

LOOMIS. It's the newest model.

QUARTERMAINE. Yes, I think that's the trouble, all those extra bits to master — anyway one of the colleges went in upside down and wouldn't come out so I had to — to abandon technology and do it all off my own bat — you know, reminiscences of my time at the House and — and anecdotes — and — you know — that sort of thing. The personal touch. But of course I ran out of steam a little, towards the end. I'm afraid. (*Laughs*).

LOOMIS. And how many turned up?

QUARTERMAINE. Oh well — about a handful.

LOOMIS. A handful!

QUARTERMAINE. A good handful.

LOOMIS. But there are meant to be twenty-three in the group that that special lecture's designed for.

QUARTERMAINE. Yes, well I think you know — it's being Friday and — and the sun shining and the Backs so lovely and the Cam jam-packed with punts and — but the ones who came were jolly interested — especially that little Italian girl — you know um — um — almost midget sized, the one with the wart —

LOOMIS. If you mean Angelina, she happens to be Greek. Her

father's an exceptionally distinguished army officer. Thomas will be very disappointed to hear about all this, St. John, he devised that lecture series himself, you know, it's quite an innovation, and if you can't keep attendances up — and then there's the question of the projector, I only hope you haven't done it any damage —

The sound of a door opening, footsteps hurrying.

and you know very well how important it is to keep classes going until at least the bell — ah, hello my dear, you've finished a trifle on the early side too, then?

ANITA (*enters, slightly breathless*). Oh, isn't it past five?

LOOMIS. Well, the bell hasn't gone yet, even in your part of the corridor — intermediary dictation, wasn't it, and how was your attendance?

ANITA. Oh, nearly a full complement, Eddie, they're a very keen lot, mostly Germans, in fact that's why I thought the bell had gone, one of them — Kurt — said he'd heard it.

LOOMIS. Good, good. (*He is not convinced, perhaps.*)

ANITA *makes to go to her locker.*

LOOMIS. My dear, have I told you what I think about your sandals?

ANITA. No, Eddie.

LOOMIS. Well, when I first saw you in them I wondered if they were quite *comme il faut*, Thomas and I had quite a thing about them.—

QUARTERMAINE. I think they're smashing.

LOOMIS. But I've been quite won around, I've come to the view that they're most fetching. Or that your feet are. Or both. (*He laughs.*)

ANITA. Thank you, Eddie.

LOOMIS. And Nigel's still in London, is he, with his co-editress?

ANITA. Yes, he comes back on Saturday or Sunday.

LOOMIS. Quite a coincidence Thomas seeing them on the train

like that, he's scarcely been out of his office this many a month, as you know — and it's all working out all right, is it?

ANITA. Yes, she's been absolutely wonderful, quite a surprise really, because when I first met Amanda at a party a few years ago I thought she was — well, absolutely charming, of course, but rather — rather feckless, if anything. But the girl who gave the party's a great friend of mine and she's always said Amanda had a good tough brain. Her boyfriend's being a great help too. He's invaluable.

LOOMIS. How odd, I had an idea you went to school with her?

ANITA (*slight hesitation*). No no — with her sister. Seraphina.

LOOMIS. Ah yes — but I was really asking about the magazine itself, how that was coming?

ANITA. Well, they're still having to delay publication because of these printers letting them down, but now they've found a new one in London — and they're getting in some really decent articles and things and — oh, they've finally settled on a title. It's going to be called *Reports.*

QUARTERMAINE. Terrific!

The bell rings.

LOOMIS. *Reports, Reports,* mmm, well, tell Nigel when he gets back that Thomas has decided to take out *two* subscriptions, one for ourselves and one for the student common room, so we'll be showing a great personal interest —

ANITA. Oh thank you, Eddie, Nigel will be so pleased —

From the garden, the sound of WINDSCAPE.

WINDSCAPE (*off*). I can't stay too long, I'm afraid, just to start you off and explain the rules — but first let's get the mallets and balls —

The voices recede.

LOOMIS (*going to the window*). Ah, the croquet's under way again, good, good, — and who's playing — ah, Piccolo and Jean-Pierre, Gisela — Teresa — Okona — Liv and Gerta — you know, I always feel that if ever our little school had to justify itself, we could do it by showing the world the spectacle of an Italian, a Frenchman, a German, a Japanese, a Swedish girl and a Belgian girl, all gathered together on an English lawn, under an English sky to play a game of croquet —

ANITA *through this has gone to her locker.*

QUARTERMAINE. Absolutely, Eddie, absolutely — croquet — I must try my hand again — haven't for years — my aunt had such a lawn, you know, and I remember, oh Lord, (*Shaking his head, laughing.*) Oh Lord, I say, I forgot, Thomas told me to tell you he was looking for you.

LOOMIS. Thomas? When?

QUARTERMAINE. Oh, just at the end of my lecture — he popped his head in.

LOOMIS. Really, St. John, I wish you'd mentioned it straight away, it would have to be something urgent for Thomas to interrupt a class — was he going back to the office?

SACKLING *enters, during this, carrying books, etc; he sports a moustache.*

QUARTERMAINE. He didn't say, Eddie.

LOOMIS. Mark, have you happened to glimpse Thomas —

SACKLING. Yes. I think he and Melanie were going up to your flat —

LOOMIS. Oh. Well, if he should come down here looking for me, tell him I've gone upstairs — and that I'll stay there so that we don't do one of our famous boxes and coxes — (*Goes out right.*)

SACKLING. Right Eddie (*Going to his locker.*)

ANITA, *during the above, has finished packing and is leaving. There is an air of desperate rush about her.*

QUARTERMAINE. Phew! He'd pretty well stopped showing up in here before the bell — wasn't he in a dodgy mood — but I say, where shall we meet, Anita, shall Mark and I come and pick you up at your place, or shall we go to Mark's place, or the foyer, or — or we could go to The Eagle — or you two could come to my place —

ANITA. Oh, I'm sorry, St. John, I completely forgot — you see I'm going to London. It suddenly occurred to me that as Nigel can't get back until tomorrow or Sunday, why not pop down and spend the weekend with him.

QUARTERMAINE. Oh what a good idea, spend the weekend in London with Nigel, much more fun than some old Ibsen thing —

SACKLING. Shouldn't you 'phone him first? I mean, he may be going out or — you know.

ANITA. I haven't got time. Anyway, I don't mind waiting for him — look, I've got to dash if I'm going to make the five-thirty — damn Eddie!

SACKLING. Oh — Anita, would you apologise to him again for my letting him down, I'll really try for the second issue —

ANITA (*rushing off*). Yes, right, I'll tell him —

SACKLING. Oh Christ! Poor old Nigel!

QUARTERMAINE. Mmmm?

SACKLING. Well, surely you know?

QUARTERMAINE. What?

SACKLING. About Nigel and Amanda Southgate. They're having a passionate affair. He only started the magazine because of her — she's got literary ambitions.

QUARTERMAINE. Oh Lord — oh, Lord, poor old Anita! But they always seemed so happy —

SACKLING. You know, St. John, you have an amazing ability not to let the world impinge on you. Anita's the unhappiest woman I know, at the moment. And has been, ever since she met Nigel. Amanda's his fifth affair in the last two years, even if the most serious. But she covers up for him, pretends it isn't happening, or tries to protect a reputation he hasn't got and probably doesn't want anyway, she's had three abortions for him to my knowledge, three, although she's desperate for children — haven't you had the slightest inkling of any of that?

QUARTERMAINE. No, but good Lord — how do *you* know? I mean —

SACKLING. Well, Nigel told me most of it, as a matter of fact.

But I'd still have thought it's perfectly obvious there was something amiss — but what I don't understand is why she's suddenly gone down to confront him. She's only survived so far by not daring to have anything out with him — she's never once mentioned even the most blatant of his infidelities, actually that's one of the things about her that drives him mad. But perhaps the thought of the two of them in London while she has to spend the weekend here — anyway, there's nothing we can do about it, is there? I haven't even got his number, so I can't warn him.

QUARTERMAINE. Don't you like Anita?

SACKLING. Of course I do. Far more than I like Nigel, as a matter of fact.

QUARTERMAINE. Oh. Oh well it all seems — all seems — I mean these things between people — people one cares for — it's hard to bear them — but, but I say, what about this evening then, I wonder if they'll take her ticket back or — anyway, how would you like to play it? Eagle or —

SACKLING. As a matter of fact, St. John, I'm going to have to bow out of the theatre, too.

QUARTERMAINE. Oh. Oh well —

SACKLING. To tell you the truth, I couldn't face it. You see, last night I went back to it again. My novel. The first time since Camelia left. And there was the old flame aflickering as strongly as ever. And if I don't get back to it again this evening — I'll — I'll — well, anyway, I'll have a rotten evening. And give you one, too, probably. Look, you haven't actually bought the tickets, have you?

QUARTERMAINE (*makes to say yes, changes his mind*). No, no, never any need to at the Arts, so don't worry about that but — but it's terrific, that you've started writing again, that's far more important than going to see some — some old Ibsen thing.

SACKLING. Thanks. And St. John, thanks also for your companionship these last weeks. It must have been bloody boring for you, having me grind on and on in my misery.

QUARTERMAINE. Lord no. I've enjoyed it enormously. Not your misery I don't mean but your — your — I say, did you get that letter, though?

SACKLING. Yes, this morning. She's allowing me a few hours tomorrow afternoon. With my son. Which is another reason I must spend this evening at the typewriter —

QUARTERMAINE. But that's wonderful, Mark. A breakthrough at last — look, when will you be back?

SACKLING. Tomorrow evening, I suppose.

QUARTERMAINE. Well, perhaps we could have lunch on Sunday or dinner or meet for a drink — and you could tell me how things went with little Tom — I'd really love to know.

During this, the sound of a door opening and closing, followed by a yelp.

MEADLE (*off*). Blast!

QUARTERMAINE. You all right, old man!

MEADLE (*he is wearing a blazer and flannels, and has a bump on his forehead, covered by a piece of sticking plaster*). Yes, yes — (*Rubbing his hand.*) It's that door-knob, a bit too close to the door-jamb — at least for my taste — (*He laughs.*) I'm always scraping my knuckles on it — hello, Mark, haven't seen you around for a bit, I suppose because you're usually gone before I finish.

SACKLING. Don't worry, I do my time. Right to the bell.

MEADLE. Oh, I didn't mean any reflection — (*He laughs.*) Good God, I only meant that I always seem to get caught by students who want to practise their English after hours too — of course it doesn't help to be carrying a converstaion piece around on your forehead — 'What 'appen 'ead, Mr Mittle?' 'Whasa matter weet de het, Meester Meetle?' 'Mister Mittle vat goes mit der hed?' (*Laughing.*) Up the corridor, down, in the classroom, in the garden — by the time I'd gone through all the details, with pantomime, landlady calling to the telephone, toe stubbing in cracked linoleum, body pitching down the stairs and bonce cracking down on tile I'd have settled for serious internal injuries instead.

SACKLING (*smiles*). Goodnight, see you both Monday, (*He goes out through the French windows.*)

QUARTERMAINE (*who has been laughing with* MEADLE). Oh, night old man, but oh, just a minute, we haven't fixed our meeting — (*Goes to the French windows and stares out.*)

MEADLE (*who has registered* SACKLING's *manner*). He's a hard chap to get to know, isn't he?

QUARTERMAINE. Who? Old Mark? Lord no — oh, well perhaps to begin with but once you do know him you can't imagine a — a better friend.

MEADLE. Oh. Well, I'll keep working on it then.

QUARTERMAINE. And of course he's been through a very bad time — and with his — his particular talent —

MEADLE. By the way, you haven't seen Thomas, have you? (*Going to his locker.*)

QUARTERMAINE. I think he's with Eddie, anyway they're looking for each other.

MEADLE. Oh. (*He nods.*)

QUARTERMAINE. I say, I've managed to get hold of some tickets for the theatre tonight. They're doing an Ibsen! Would you like to come?

MEADLE. To tell you the truth, Ibsen's not quite my cup of tea, thanks, but anyway as a matter of fact Oko-Ri's taking me out to dinner tonight with the rest of the boys.

QUARTERMAINE. Oko — what?

MEADLE. Ri. Oko-Ri. My Japanese chum.

QUARTERMAINE. Oh, old baldy, you mean? Taking you out to dinner — well, that's — that's — I didn't know you'd hit it off so well with them, after that business —

MEADLE. Well, I never thought they'd made me skid deliberately — and we've had lots of good laughs about it since — now that I'm on their wave-length — Oko-Ri's got a spendid

sense of humour. Loves a drink too, I gather, from some of
their jokes.

QUARTERMAINE. Oh, well, you'll have a good evening then —

MEADLE. It's really just to say thank you for all the extra hours
I've put in with them. They left it to me to decide where we'd
go, and I've chosen that French place that's just opened
opposite Trinity, Eddie and Thomas were saying it's very good
— I'm a bit worried about that, though, I hope it's not too
expensive — I had a feeling they hesitated slightly or Oko-Ri
did, he's very much the man in charge. One has to keep
sensitive to these things — but of course once I'd asked for it,
it was too late to change — but I'd better get back if I'm going
to meet them later — did I tell you my landlady's just offered
me another room as a bedroom letting me keep the bedroom
I've got now as a study-cum-sitting-room, so I'm virtually
ending up with a little suite of my own, and all for just another
twenty-five shillings, for five pounds in all.

QUARTERMAINE. Good Lord. And to think I'm paying six
pounds for my pokey little room — how on earth did you
manage that, Derek?

MEADLE. I think it's because I remind her of her son, being the
same age almost, and he never bothers to write or come to
visit, as far as I can make out.

QUARTERMAINE. Golly, I should have a go at Mrs Harris, see if
I can remind her of her son, if she has one, although if he's
anything like her I hope I don't, eh? Anyway, you certainly do
land on your feet, old man, don't you?

MEADLE. Well — (*He laughs.*) sometimes on my head, eh?
Anyway, I'd better get back, (*Putting on his bicycle clips.*)
I've asked Oko-Ri and his boys to initiate my suite, with a
bottle of whisky, before our dinner, and I've still got some
furniture to move — I'd ask you to come along too, but it's
not really my invitation —

QUARTERMAINE. Oh — (*He gestures.*)

The sound of a door opening and closing; feet.

MEADLE (*going out*). Oh. Here. Let me give you a hand with those, Melanie —

MELANIE (*off*). No, it's quite all right, I've got them —

MEADLE (*off*). Well, let me just take this one —

MELANIE. No, no, really — there's no need —

The sound of books dropping on the floor.

MEADLE (*off*). Oh, sorry, Melanie —

MELANIE (*irritably*). Oh — really! I had them perfectly well — and Thomas has just lent me that one with great warnings to be careful, it's a rare edition —

MEADLE *comes on stage, carrying a distinguished volume.*

MELANIE (*coming on stage, carrying a briefcase, exercise books and further books*). If you could just put it on the table —

MEADLE. What, here do you mean?

MELANIE. Have either of you seen Eddie? Thomas has been looking for him.

QUARTERMAINE. Now what did Eddie say — oh yes, that he was going to wait for Thomas in the — in the office, it must have been.

MELANIE. Oh, well that's where Thomas has gone — he took me down into the cellar to find the book — it took him longer than he thought and he got worried that Eddie would go into one of his panics, and be in and out of every room in the school — you know how clever they are at just missing each other — so you're the last two then, are you?

QUARTERMAINE. Yes, well apart from old Henry, that is, he's playing croquet —

MELANIE. Is he? Jolly good! (*She goes to her locker.*)

MEADLE (*who has been looking through the book*). No, no damage done, Melanie — (*He looks at his watch.*) so Thomas is in the office, is he?

MELANIE. Yes, why, what do you want him for?

MEADLE. Oh — well — well actually he said something about

seeing if he could get me some extra pronunciation classes —
my rent has just gone up, you see, so I really rather need the
extra bobs. (*He laughs.*)

MELANIE. I wouldn't go disturbing him now, if I were you, he's
had a particularly fraught day. He's got a dreadful headache.
The only person he'll want to see is Eddie.

MEADLE. Oh. Well, in that case — goodnight, Melanie.

MELANIE. Goodnight — oh, that reminds me, I'd be very grateful
if you'd stop putting your bicycle against the wall just where I
park my car — there's not enough room for both.

MEADLE. Oh, sorry about that — right Melanie — well, see you
Monday then.

QUARTERMAINE. See you Monday, old man.

MEADLE *goes out through the French windows.*

MELANIE. I really think I'd get on much better with Mr Meadle
if he didn't try so hard to get on with me. Still, I really had no
right to stop him from seeing Thomas — not my business at
all. It's just that he's spent the whole afternoon on the
telephone because of that wretched Jap — the big, bald one,
you know — apparently he got drunk and ran amok in that
new French restaurant last night, and the owners are
demanding damages and threatening to call the police, if he
shows up again, and then one of the other Japanese turned up
at lunch-time to book a table for tonight — Goodness knows
what's going to happen if the bald one appears too.

MEADLE (*meanwhile, off*). 'Night, Henry, see you Monday.

WINDSCAPE (*off*). Oh. 'Night Derek. Have a good weekend.

MEADLE (*off*). Thanks, Henry — same to you.

MELANIE (*listens alertly to this*). Still, apparently he works
very hard at his teaching, from all accounts, Thomas and
Eddie are both rather thrilled with him — well, St. John, and
what are your plans for the weekend, something on the boil,
I'll bet!

QUARTERMAINE. Oh, well I thought I might take in a show

tonight — that Ibsen thing at the Arts —

MELANIE. Isn't it *The Cherry Orchard*?

QUARTERMAINE. Oh, is it? Well — something like that. And then a bite of supper, I suppose. I might try that French place in fact. Might be rather — rather amusing. (*He laughs.*)

MELANIE. It must be jolly nice being a bachelor and having the weekend before you. Especially in Cambridge. Well, I'd better get on with this. I don't think Thomas really wants me to take it off the premises. (*She pulls book towards her.*)

QUARTERMAINE. Oh. Righto. (*He begins to wander up and down, gaze out of the French windows etc.*)

MELANIE *is writing, glancing occasionally at him. She is, in fact, anxious for him to be gone. There are occasional cries and sounds of* WINDSCAPE'S *voice from the garden, to which* MELANIE *responds by lifting her head, or stopping writing.*

QUARTERMAINE. I say, Melanie — do you like *The Cherry Orchard*?

MELANIE. Loathe it.

QUARTERMAINE. Oh. Why?

MELANIE. All that Russian gloom and doom and people shooting themselves from loneliness and depression and that sort of thing. But then mother says I don't understand comedy. I expect she's right.

QUARTERMAINE. How is mother?

MELANIE. Oh, top hole, thanks. (*Automatically.*)

QUARTERMAINE. Well, if there's ever anything I can do — you know — if she wants company when you want to go out —

MELANIE. That's very thoughtful of you, St. John, thank you.

QUARTERMAINE. No, no — I'd enjoy it. I say, that is an impressive tome old Thomas has lent you, what are you copying out exactly?

MELANIE. Recipes. This one's for roasted swan.

QUARTERMAINE. Oh. For a dinner party?

MELANIE. No, no, St. John it's for my British Life and Institutions lot, to give them some idea of a Medieval banquet. Swans are protected birds, you know, these days.

QUARTERMAINE. Oh yes, of course they are. (*He laughs.*) Fancy thinking you'd give them for a — a — oh Lord! But aren't they the most — most beautiful creatures. I was looking at one — oh, just the other day, you know — on the Cam — drifting behind a punt — and they were all shouting and drinking champagne and — and it was just drifting behind them — so calm — and I remember there used to be oh! a dozen or so — they came every year to a pond near my aunt's — when I was — was — and I could hear their wings — great wings beating — in the evenings when I was lying in bed — it could be quite — quite frightening even after I knew what was making the noise — and then there they'd be — a dozen of them or so — drifting — drifting around the next morning — and it was hard to imagine — their long necks twining and their way of drifting — all that — that power — those wings beating — I wonder where they went to. I'd like to know more about them really. Where they go, what they — they —

MELANIE. St. John, please don't think me fearfully rude, but I must try and finish this and I can't write and talk at the same time, you see.

QUARTERMAINE. What? Oh — oh sorry, Melanie, no, you're quite right, I can't either. Anyway, I ought to be getting on —

MELANIE. Yes, with such a full evening. I do hope you enjoy it.

QUARTERMAINE. Well — well, 'night Melanie, see you Monday. And don't forget about your mother — any time —

MELANIE. I won't, St. John, goodnight.

QUARTERMAINE *goes.*

MELANIE *sits, not writing, as*

QUARTERMAINE (*off*). I say, Henry, any chance of a game?

WINDSCAPE (*off*). Actually, I'm just finishing I'm afraid — perhaps next week.

QUARTERMAINE (*off*). Right, I'll hold you to that. See you

Monday. Oh, by the way, if you want any baby-sitting done
during the weekend, I'll try and make myself available —

WINDSCAPE (*off*). Righto, I'll put it to Fanny — I know she's
quite keen to see the *Uncle Vanya* at the Arts — perhaps
tomorrow night —

QUARTERMAINE. A votre disposition. (*Off.*) 'Night.

WINDSCAPE. 'Night.

MELANIE, *during this, has got up, and gone to the French
windows.*

WINDSCAPE (*off*). Oh, well played, Piccolo, well played
Jean-Piere — beautiful lies both — I have to go now I'm afraid,
but you're obviously learning very quickly all of you — don't
forget to put the mallets and the balls back in the sheds —
goodnight, goodnight.

*Replies, in the appropriate accents, of: 'Goodnight,
Mr Windscape', etc.*

MELANIE, *during the latter part of this, hurries back to the
table, sits down, pretends to continue transcribing.*

WINDSCAPE *enters through the French windows. He stops
on seeing* MELANIE, *braces himself, then enters properly,
jovially.*

WINDSCAPE. Hello Melanie, my dear, I thought everyone had
gone.

MELANIE. How are they taking to the croquet?

WINDSCAPE. At the moment they find it a bit sedate, I think,
but another time or two around and they'll discover just how
much — how much incivility is possible on our tranquil English
lawns — but — but what are you up to? (*Coming to look over
her shoulder.*) Isn't that Cussons' *A Culinary History of
England*? I've only seen it in a library before, and what are you
transcribing — roasted swan, for British Life and Institutions, is
it? But you know Melanie, that's rather a good idea — as a way
of teaching them some social history I mean — you'll be able
to compare dishes from different strata of society at the same
period, and then at different periods — why, you could work

through a whole chronology of meals, from Medieval banquets of — of roasted swan and no doubt boar and venison and guinea fowls right up to — to the modern dinner of frozen hamburgers, frozen chips and frozen peas — and — and — thus illustrating one aspect of our culture's advance, eh, from a very few eating splendidly to almost everybody getting hideously fed — and — and — why good heavens, see where it takes you — a consideration of meals as symbolic functions and domestic rituals — you could bring D.H. Lawrence in there, as *Sons and Lovers* is a set text, isn't it — and — and not forgetting of course all the semantic fun, the differences in meaning between lunches, luncheons, teas, high teas, suppers, dinners — and of course what they indicate as a kind of code about class — and — and — the illustrations, not only literary, Shakespeare alone — Banquo's ghost — Antony and Cleopatra — Titus Andronicus! almost every play, and the novels — but also paintings, lithographs, Hogarth — (*He checks himself from going on*.) good gracious you've really hit on something there, Melanie.

MELANIE (*who has been gazing at him adoringly*). And all I thought I'd hit on was a way of attracting a little interest — especially from those three rather scowly French girls — but then how like you, Henry, to take up my copying out an old recipe and turn it into an intellectual adventure.

WINDSCAPE (*laughs, embarrassed*). Oh just a few — just a few thoughts — letting myself get carried away as usual, and I really ought to be sorting myself out — I promised Fanny I'd be home by six — now where's my briefcase — ah, yes — and a pile of unseens I seem to remember — (*Going to his locker*.) to be marked by Monday —

MELANIE. How is Fanny?

WINDSCAPE. Oh, very well thanks, very well — a bit tired in the evenings, what with the children on the one hand and her two hours voluntary with the OAPs — but she's enjoying every minute of her day —

MELANIE. Good! — And the children — all well?

WINDSCAPE. Oh yes — they're fine! Susan's a little tense at the moment, actually, with her 'O' levels — a pity she's taking them so early, I think, but she insists — she's in with a particularly bright lot and doesn't want to fall behind or let herself down so she works away until all hours. Quite often after Fanny and I have gone to bed. But she's developing quite an interest in — in — well, philosophical speculation, I suppose it is, really — the other evening — (*Bending during this to put on his clips.*) she suddenly insisted — in the middle of supper — she'd been very quiet until then — she suddenly insisted that we couldn't prove that other people existed — and that perhaps when we thought about them or remembered them or saw and heard them even — we were actually just making them up — and of course I took her up on this and attempted to explain how it is we do know that other people exist, including people we don't even know exist, if you follow — (*Laughing.*) and she kept saying 'But you can't prove it, Daddy, you can't actually prove it!' until I found myself getting quite tangled in my own arguments — and trying to remember whether there is an irrefutable answer to solipsism — Fanny had to rescue me in the end by calling me up to read to little Fanny and Ben —

MELANIE. I've always thought she was the one who takes most after you.

WINDSCAPE. Yes, yes — perhaps she does, perhaps she does — I'm afraid I rather like to think so anyway — (*He laughs.*) but you haven't seen them for ages have you, you really must come over sometime soon — Fanny would love to see you again. We all would.

MELANIE. That would be lovely.

WINDSCAPE. I'll get Fanny to give you a ring over the weekend or —

MELANIE. Good.

WINDSCAPE. Right — well, oh, by the way, I've been meaning to ask — how is the day-nurse working out, Nurse — Nurse — with the name out of Dickens.

MELANIE. Grimes. Well enough so far — she seems a very efficient, cheerful, little soul — a little too cheerful for my taste perhaps, as apparently she belongs to one of those peculiar revivalist sects that seem to be springing up all over the place now — you know, meeting in each other's homes and chanting prayers and dancing about in their love of God — at least that's how she describes it — but Mother seems to like her.

WINDSCAPE. Well, that's the main thing, isn't it?

MELANIE. Yes. Yes it is.

WINDSCAPE. Well do give her my — my very best — see you Monday, Melanie, my dear.

MELANIE. See you Monday Henry.

WINDSCAPE, *carrying papers, books, etc, goes off left. The sound of the door closing.*

MELANIE *sits. She lets out a sudden wail, and then in a sort of frenzy, tears at the page of the book from which she's been copying, sobbing. She checks herself, as: the sound of the door opening.*

WINDSCAPE (*laughing*). What on earth can I be thinking of — going off with all these in my arms and leaving my briefcase behind — I do that sort of thing more and more now — perhaps it's premature senility — (*Entering, going to the briefcase, shovelling the papers and books in.*) or did I get switched on to the wrong track and think I was going off to teach a class — I must have as I went out that way — (*Looks at her smiling. A little pause.*) Melanie — Melanie — (*He hesitates, then goes to her, leaving the briefcase on the desk.*) Is something the matter?

MELANIE. I'm sorry — I'm sorry — but I've got to talk — talk to someone —

WINDSCAPE. What is it?

MELANIE. She hates me, you see.

WINDSCAPE. Who?

MELANIE. Mother.

WINDSCAPE. Oh Melanie, I'm sure that's not — not — why do you think she does?

MELANIE. She says I've abandoned her. Betrayed her. When I
come back in the evenings she won't speak to me. She sits
silent for hours, while I prepare supper and chatter at her, and
then when I've got her to the table she refuses to eat. Since
that second attack she can only work one side of her mouth,
but she can eat perfectly well. She says Nurse Grimes feeds her
and so I should too, but when I try she lets the food fall out
of her mouth, and — and stares at me with such malevolence,
until suddenly she'll say something — something utterly — last
night she said 'It's not my fault you've spent your life in my
home. I've never wanted you here, but as you're too stupid to
make an intelligent career, and too unattractive to make any
reasonable man a wife, I was prepared to accept the
responsibility for you. And now you refuse to pay your debt.
Oh, sharper than a serpent's tooth . . .' And coming out of the
side of her mouth, in a hoarse whisper, like a — like a gangster
in one of those films. And she wets herself too. From spite.
She never does it with Nurse Grimes, of course. Only with me.
She says that as I'm behaving like a neglectful parent, she'll
behave like a neglected child. The only child I'll ever have.
And she gives Nurse Grimes things — things that belong to
me or she knows I love that we've had for years — the
buttons from Daddy's uniform or the other day a silly
lithograph of a donkey that's hung in my room since I was
ten — of course Nurse Grimes gives them back but — but and
the worst thing is I'm beginning to hate her, to hate going
home or when I'm there have such dreadful feelings — because
the thought of years — it could be years apparently — years of
this — and so wishing she would have another attack and die
now — too dreadful — too dreadful — almost imagining myself
doing something —

WINDSCAPE. You mustn't blame yourself for that, Melanie, you
mustn't. It's only natural — and healthy, probably, even. But
I'm so sorry she's — I had no idea — what can one say? I know
— we both know — what a remarkable woman she was, and I
suppose that the indignity of finding herself increasingly
incapacitated and the — the fear of what's going to happen to
her — I suppose when it comes to it, when we come to our
ends some of us are — well, all the anger and despair turn to

cruelty — and of course you're the only one —

MELANIE. I know. But I can't give up my teaching, Henry, I can't. Your getting me this job was the best thing that ever happened to me — of course she always despised it — even when she was well she thought it — thought it — having been a Professor herself — but I love it and — and I've got to think of myself now. Haven't I?

WINDSCAPE. Yes. Yes, of course you have. Finally, one always must. I wish I could give you some comfort, my dear.

MELANIE. You do, Henry. Your just being here and my knowing that you — that you care about me makes all the difference. All the difference. It always has (*She begins to cry.*) Oh what a fool I was not to — not to marry you when you asked me — all those years ago — I keep thinking of it now — and what Mother said about your being too young and not knowing what you were doing — and — and blighting your career — of course I'm happy that you're so happy — I wouldn't have been able to make you as happy, but even then she was my enemy — my real enemy — I'm sorry, I'm sorry — (*Sobbing.*)

WINDSCAPE (*hesitates, then with reluctance puts his arms around her.*) There there, my dear, there there — mustn't think of the past — it's the — the future — the future — there there —

The telephone rings.

(*After a moment.*) Perhaps I'd better — perhaps I'd better — um — (*Releasing himself, he picks up the telephone.*) Hello. Oh Hello Nigel, yes it is! No she's gone I'm afraid — at least I think she has — have you seen Anita in the last half hour —

MELANIE, *now handkerchiefing her tears, shakes her head.*

Melanie hasn't seen her either so I'm fairly sure — yes, of course I will. (*He listens.*) You're 'phoning from Liverpool Street and you're about to catch the 6.13 so you'll be home before eight, right, got that but as I say — have you tried her at home — oh, well, if she's going to the theatre perhaps she's gone straight there, eh? but if Melanie or I do see her by any unlikely — yes, right, goodbye — and oh, Nigel, good luck with your first issue, Fanny and I and everybody we know are so looking forward to it — have you decided what you're going to call it by the way? Really? Well, that sounds — that really sounds most — most — yes — goodbye. (*He hangs up.*) That was Nigel — for Anita — as you probably realized and — and anyway she's certainly left, hasn't she — Nigel says she said she was going to the theatre — so — so — I suppose the Arts — *The Three Sisters,* isn't it? — such a beautiful play although not — not my favourite — which will always be *The Seagull.* Apparently they're going to call the magazine *Reports,* by the way, I'm not sure I care too much for *Reports,* do you? (*He stares hopelessly at* MELANIE, *who has somewhat recovered herself.*) You must come around, Melanie and have a real — a real talk with Fanny — take you out of yourself — away from your problems —

MELANIE. Thank you, Henry.

WINDSCAPE. No, we'd love to see you, I'll get her to ring you. All right? And now I must — I really must — (*Looking at the clock.*) I promised Susan I'd help her with her maths, and then I've got to listen to Ben doing a Chopin piece, he's going to perform it at the school concert, really rather too advanced, but still, and there's little Fanny's bed-time read — I'm trying to get her on to Walter De La Mare but he hasn't really taken yet — so — so —

MELANIE. Yes, you must get back.

WINDSCAPE. Yes. See you Monday, my dear.

MELANIE. Monday, Henry.

WINDSCAPE *looks around vaguely for a moment, then goes out through the French windows.*

MELANIE *stands for a moment, then sees the briefcase, registers it, takes it to* WINDSCAPE's *locker, puts it in, goes back to the book, looks down at it, tries futilely to sort it out, pressing the page flat with her hand, then goes to collect her briefcase, etc. As she does so, the sound of violent quarrelling, in assorted tongues, off, over the croquet: 'No, you cannot — Mr Windscape said . . .' etc.*

MELANIE *pauses to listen, then as the voices continue, then fade, the sound of the door, off left, opening.*

MELANIE. Oh, hello Eddie! (*Brightly.*)

LOOMIS. He's not here then — I can't make out — I've been everywhere, everywhere, up to the flat, all the class-rooms and in the office — and the 'phone going all the time about some of our Japanese and that French restaurant, and they're not even French, it turns out, they're from Wiltshire — and I don't know what Thomas has said to them, I didn't even know about it — he knows I can't deal with that sort of thing — and he's booked a table for the two of us tonight at their request, forcing us to take responsibility, I don't see what it's got to do with the school if a few Japanese can't hold their drink, I don't know why he agreed — it really is all too —

MELANIE. Now Eddie. Now. (*Going to him.*) You mustn't worry. You'll make yourself ill, and it's not worth it. Why don't you go upstairs to the flat and have a rest, I'm sure it'll all sort itself out, you know Thomas, he'll get it completely under control, he always does, in the end.

LOOMIS. Yes, yes, of course you're right, my dear, thank you, thank you. And a little rest — and I'll try and make Thomas have one, too —

MELANIE. That's right, Eddie, you both need it — oh, and would you give this back to him when you see him, and tell him I'm terribly sorry (*as she collects her briefcase and hands LOOMIS the book.*) a page of it seems to have got torn — our Mr Meadle insisted on snatching it out of my hands and then dropped it — he was only trying to be helpful of course — but you know how clumsy he is —

LOOMIS. Oh — oh dear, Cussons — one of our favourite books, Thomas will find it hard to forgive Meadle — well — have a good weekend my dear, and bless you. (*They go off.*)

MELANIE. Thank you Eddie. (*Off.*)

LOOMIS (*footsteps off, then he stops*). Oh, and by the way, how's mother?

MELANIE. Oh, top hole, thanks Eddie.

LOOMIS. Good, good. (*The sound of the door shutting.*)

There is a pause. QUARTERMAINE *enters through the French windows. He looks around him, stands for a moment, then sweeps his left leg, vaguely, as —*

Lights.

Curtain.

ACT TWO

Scene One

The following year, towards summer. It is a Monday morning, about 9.30.

There have been a few improvements, different perhaps; a record player, with a record rack consisting of poetry readings and Shakespeare plays. There is also a large new tape-recorder, sophisticated for the period.

QUARTERMAINE is seated, with his feet up, staring ahead.

WINDSCAPE enters through the French windows, carrying a briefcase, smoking a pipe, wearing bicycle clips.

WINDSCAPE. Hello St. John. (*He goes to his locker.*)

QUARTERMAINE (*doesn't respond at first, then takes in WINDSCAPE*). Oh, hello — um (*He thinks.*) Henry.

WINDSCAPE (*turns, looks at him*). Deep in thought?

QUARTERMAINE. Mmmm? Oh. No no — just — just — you know.

WINDSCAPE. Ah. Did you have a good half-term?

QUARTERMAINE. Oh. Yes thanks. Yes.

WINDSCAPE. What did you do? Did you go away? (*Going to his locker.*)

QUARTERMAINE. Well, I — I — no, I stayed here.

WINDSCAPE. Here!

QUARTERMAINE. Yes.

WINDSCAPE. Oh, in Cambridge, you mean? Just for a moment I thought you meant actually *here* — in this room — I think perhaps because the last time I saw you, you were sitting in exactly the same place in very much that position — as if you haven't moved all week.

QUARTERMAINE. Oh. (*He laughs.*) But I say — good to be back, isn't it?

WINDSCAPE. Well, I could have done with a little longer myself.

QUARTERMAINE (*watches* WINDSCAPE *at the locker.*) I say, Henry, what did you do for the half?

WINDSCAPE. Mmmm? Oh nothing very exciting really, we packed ourselves into the caravan and took ourselves off to a spot we'd heard about in Norfolk —

QUARTERMAINE. That sounds terrific!

WINDSCAPE. Yes — yes — well, the trouble was that it rained fairly steadily — all week, in fact — so we didn't get out as much as we would have liked — a shame really as among other things we were hoping that a few jaunts would cheer Susan up.

QUARTERMAINE. Oh — is she a bit low then?

WINDSCAPE. Yes yes — well she's still brooding over her 'O' level results — we keep telling her that at her age six positive passes — I mean Bs and Cs — is jolly good — but she seems to feel she's let herself down — but I'll tell you what we did see — it really was most — extraordinary — one morning at about six it was, I was up trying to plug the leak — it was right over little Fanny's bunk — and so she was awake and so was Ben — and Susan hadn't slept at all — so it was all rather — rather fraught. with tempers fraying — but Fanny she'd gone outside to the loo, as a matter of fact — and suddenly she called us — all of us — told us to put on our wellies and macs and come out and look — and we did — and there — silhouetted against the sky was the most — the most —

MEADLE *enters through the French windows in bicycle clips, carrying a briefcase.*

MEADLE. Greetings, Henry, St. John.

QUARTERMAINE. Hello, old chap.

WINDSCAPE. Hello, Derek. Have a good holiday?

MEADLE. Yes, thanks, Henry, very, very good indeed. What about you? (*Goes to his locker, taking off his clips, etc.*)

WINDSCAPE. Yes, I was just telling St. John, we went to Norfolk, a little wet, but there really was one very remarkable — well, moment is all it amounted to really. In temporal terms.

MEADLE. Sounds marvellous. Thomas isn't around yet, is he?

WINDSCAPE. He wasn't in the office when I came through, have you seen him, St. John?

QUARTERMAINE. Mmmm?

WINDSCAPE. Thomas. Have you seen him?

QUARTERMAINE. No no — but I expect he's here somewhere. Up in their flat or — or down in their office but I say — I say, Dennis, did you have a good holiday?

MEADLE. Who's Dennis, St. John? (*He laughs.*)

QUARTERMAINE. Mmmm?

WINDSCAPE. You said Dennis, instead of Derek. And he's already said he had a very good holiday.

QUARTERMAINE. Oh. What did you do?

MEADLE. I went to Sheffield, as a matter of fact.

WINDSCAPE. Sheffield, I know it well, Fanny and I went there the year before Susan was born, we were doing a tour of out-of-the-way urban domestic architecture, I've got great affection for Sheffield, what were *you* doing there?

MEADLE. Um — oh. Attending my aunt's funeral, as a matter of fact.

QUARTERMAINE. What?

WINDSCAPE. Oh Derek, I'm so sorry. How upsetting for you.

MEADLE. Yes, it was. Very. Very.

WINDSCAPE. But actually when I asked you earlier, you did say — I suppose it was merely social reflex — that you'd had a good half-term —

MEADLE. Yes, well actually I met someone there I used to know. And I managed to see quite a lot of her. That was the good part of it. Not my aunt's death, I need hardly say. (*He laughs.*)

WINDSCAPE. Ah.

QUARTERMAINE. Who was she?

MEADLE. Oh, just a girl St John, — we were at Hull University together, as a matter of fact, she was doing the library course but we — we lost contact, for various reasons. Although I hadn't forgotten her. And when I was in Sheffield I had to take back all my poor aunt's books. And there she was. Behind the counter.

QUARTERMAINE. What was she doing there?

MEADLE. Well, stamping the books in and out of course. What do you think she was doing? (*With a mitigating laugh.*)

WINDSCAPE. Oh don't worry about St. John, one of his absent days, eh St. John, but how nice for you to bump into her like that, especially under those circumstances, eh?

MEADLE. Yes, I can't tell you what a — a blessing it turned out to be. As soon as she was off work she'd come over and sit with me and my uncle, and on a couple of evenings when I had to go out and console some of my aunt's friends, she came and sat with him anyway, by herself. He's very keen on football, but he can't follow it in the newspapers as his eyesight's nearly gone and they're too quick for him on the radio. So she'd read out all the teams and their scores. Which was very tiring for her, as she's got quite a serious speech impediment.

WINDSCAPE. What a nice girl she sounds, eh, St. John?

QUARTERMAINE. What, Henry?

WINDSCAPE. What a nice girl Derek's friend sounds.

QUARTERMAINE. Oh — oh yes, terrific, terrific. Um, tell me — tell me — what — what are her legs like?

MEADLE. What!

WINDSCAPE. Good heavens, St. John, what an extraordinary question!

QUARTERMAINE. Oh yes, — oh — I'm sorry — I was just trying to imagine — I have a sort of thing about girls' legs, you see.

(*He laughs apologetically.*) I can't stand them if they're dumpy
or — (*He thinks.*) stumpy.

MEADLE. Well, let's just say, shall we, St. John, (*Manifestly
exercising smiling control.*) that Daphne's legs happen to be
my sort of legs. Will that help you to imagine them?

QUARTERMAINE. Your sort of legs. (*He looks at* MEADLE's
legs.)

MEADLE. The sort of legs I happen to like. But I don't want to
dilate on the subject of Daphne's legs (*He laughs.*) at least just
at the moment — look, St. John, I wonder if you'd mind,
there's a matter I was very much hoping to have a conversation
with Henry about. As a matter of fact, it's rather urgent.

QUARTERMAINE. Oh. No. Sorry. Go ahead.

MEADLE. Well the thing is, St. John, it's — it's of a confidential
nature.

QUARTERMAINE. Oh — oh well, I'll go and have a little stroll
then, in the garden. (*Getting up.*) To tell you the truth my
head feels a little — a little — as if it could do with some air.

MEADLE. Thanks very much, St. John, very decent of you.

QUARTERMAINE (*going off*). Oh, not at all — but I say — I say
— (*Going out.*) what a beautiful morning! (*He goes.*)

MEADLE (*smiling*). You know, I can't help wondering sometimes
about old Quartermaine. I can't imagine a more charming
fellow but from the students' point of view — do you know
what one of the advanced Swedes was telling me just before
half-term —

WINDSCAPE (*interrupting*). I think it would be better really —
really much better — if we didn't find ourselves talking about
a colleague and a friend — I know that your concern is
entirely — entirely disinterested, but — but — these little
conflabs *can* do unintended harm. I hope you don't mind my
— my — pointing it out.

MEADLE. Not at all, Henry, you're quite right, one can't be too
careful, needless to say I meant no — no slur on St. John —

WINDSCAPE. I know you didn't, I know you didn't. But now.
you said you had something urgent —

MEADLE. Yes, well, the thing is — well look, I've been here a
year now, Henry, and Thomas said when I started that it
wouldn't be·long before I made permanent — and yet here I
am, you see, still on part-time. The only one of the staff on
part-time, as it happens. (*He laughs.*)

WINDSCAPE. And part-time isn't really very satisfactory for
you, then?

MEADLE. Well, no, it isn't, Henry, frankly. I get paid one
pound two and sixpence for every hour I teach.

WINDSCAPE. But surely Dennis —

MEADLE. Derek. (*He laughs.*) Quartermaine seems to have
started you off on Dennis —

WINDSCAPE. Oh good heavens, I'm so sorry, *Derek* — but one
pound two and sixpence an hour isn't such a bad rate, is it?

MEADLE. Ah yes, Henry, but you see I don't get paid during
the vacations, you see. I only get paid by the hour for the
hours I'm allowed to do, while the rest of the staff get paid
an annual salary. So even though I'm currently doing twice
as many hours again as everybody else, I in fact get slightly
less than half of what everybody else gets, over the year. I
mean, take this half-term we've just had, Henry, a week of
paid holiday for everybody else but a week of no money at
all for me, it was just luck that my aunt died in it, or I might
have.had to miss an earning week to go to her funeral and
sort out my uncle you see. — And last Christmas, well, I've
kept this very quiet, Henry, but last Christmas I had to be a
post-man. (*He laughs.*)

WINDSCAPE. Oh dear!

MEADLE. Yes, and let me tell you it wasn't simply the work,
Henry — being up at six, and trudging through the snow and
sleet we had the whole of those three weeks — it was also the
sheer embarrassment. Twice during my second round I nearly
bumped into some students. I only got away with it because I
kept my head lowered and once Thomas himself went right

past me in the car — it was a miracle he didn't see me, especially as I'd slipped on some ice and I was actually lying on the pavement with the letters scattered everywhere — and now the summer holiday's looming ahead — I simply don't know how I'm going to get through that. Or at least I do. I've already sent in my application to be an Entertainments Officer at one of those holiday camps in Hayling Island.

WINDSCAPE. Oh dear!

MEADLE. Yes. And now that Daphne's back in the picture — well you probably gathered from what I said that we're pretty serious about each other — and I don't want to keep her waiting around with a long engagement — there's been a lot of tragedy in that family, Henry.

WINDSCAPE. Oh dear!

MEADLE. Yes, I won't go into it, if you don't mind. Not that Daphne tries to conceal it. She's too straightforward for that.

WINDSCAPE. Well, she really does sound a most — a most remarkable —

MEADLE. Yes, I consider myself a very, very lucky man. So what do you think, Henry — I know how much Eddie and Thomas respect you — I'm going to try and nab Thomas for a few minutes this morning — how should I go about it, with him?

WINDSCAPE. Well, Derek, I think there's no doubt that you have a very strong case. Very strong. And as we all know, Thomas and Eddie are very fair, always. I know they'd respond most sympathetically — most sympathetically — to all that you've told me about yourself and Deirdre —

MEADLE. Daphne, actually. (*Smiling.*)

WINDSCAPE. Daphne — I'm sorry, Daphne of course —

The sound of the door opening: footsteps.

SACKLING (*off*). 'Morning. (*He enters somewhat jauntily, his moustache now accompanied by a beard.*) Henry — Derek —

WINDSCAPE. Oh hello, Mark, good holiday?

MEADLE. You didn't notice if Thomas was in his office as you went by, did you?

SACKLING. Yes, he was. Just come down. I like the chin. A comparatively unexplored area, isn't it, if we exclude the puffy nose from falling over the croquet hoop just before summer, how did you come by it, not shaving, I trust.

MEADLE (*who has been getting up*). Oh, I'd forgotten about that — no, no, not shaving, don't worry — (*Attempting a chuckle.*) I'll tell you all about it later — and thanks, Henry, for your advice. It was most helpful —

WINDSCAPE. Oh, not at all, I'm glad if — if —

MEADLE *goes out, during this, and as the door closes:*

WINDSCAPE. Oh — oh good heavens — Derek! Oh —

SACKLING. What's the matter?

WINDSCAPE. I think we had a slight misunderstanding — he's under the impression that I was advising him to go and see Thomas about being put on a more — a more permanent basis — and the truth is I was going on to explain to him that in spite of the — the strong claim he has — he should — well, in my view anyway — hold his horses for the moment — Thomas is under a bit of strain, you see, with all the recent renovation expenses and now the sudden drop in student in-take — this business of the Japanese suddenly deserting has really hit us very hard — so in fact it's the worst possible moment for Meadle — I was going to try and divert him to Eddie — I do sometimes feel, strictly between ourselves, that it *is* hard on him as the only part-time teacher — and we must be careful in the staff-room not to show any — any — well, make fun of him more than is perhaps — under the circumstances — if you see, Mark.

SACKLING. Oh, I shouldn't worry about Meadle. (*He's been at the locker during all the above.*) Even St. John's observed that he's one of those people who always lands on his feet — even if he damages a toe in the process. The thing is to make sure it's his and not yours. Well, Henry, peace-maker, apostle and saint, what sort of half did you have?

WINDSCAPE. Oh, we did the usual sort of thing, took the

caravan to a spot near the Broads. The weather wasn't too splendid but as I was telling — St. John, I think it was — there was one rather exceptional experience. To tell you the truth I've never seen anything quite like it. Fanny actually wrote a small sort of prose poem about it.

SACKLING. Really? I didn't know Fanny wrote! But on that subject — listen — I must tell you. I've finished.

WINDSCAPE. Finished?

SACKLING. My novel, old cheese.

WINDSCAPE. Oh Mark — well, congratulations, congratulations!

SACKLING. Thanks Henry. I knew *you'd* know what it means to me, I'd rather you kept it to yourself for the moment — for superstitious reasons, as it's still only the first draft. But the point is I feel — in my guts — that it's the first draft of the final version and damned near the thing itself, actually. Because of the way it happened, you see. What I did was — I put everything I'd previously written — a total by the way of 3,643 pages — into a box and lugged it into the cellar and started again. Completely from scratch. Just me, the typewriter and a carton of paper. I was actually quite — quite frightened. But it was all perfectly simple. No strain. No effort. Almost no thought. Just a steady untaxing continuous flow of creation. For a whole week. It was the nearest I've come, will probably ever come, to a mystical experience.

WINDSCAPE. I envy you. I once tried to write a novel — but as Fanny said my forte — if I have a forte — (*He laughs.*)

SACKLING. The thing is, though — the thing is -- it proves to *me* that I'm a novelist. The doubts I've had since Camelia left — and worst of all, the envy! I'd read the reviews and see the photographs of other novelists — the real ones, who'd been published — some of them people I knew, had been up with — God, there's a man at Trinity — an absolute imbecile — his *second* novel came out last month, well received too — and when I saw his face in the middle of some interview he'd given — the same imbecile face, with a smirk added — that I used to see opposite me in Hall I — I — well, I'd better not go into what I wanted to do to him. And all those women that are getting published everywhere — everyone, everyone but me, that's what I began to think — as if they'd got something, through some genetic accident — like an extra gland or double joints — that I hadn't. And so they could do it, again and again — while I was working away like some — some drudge — some lunatic drudge who'd given up his wife and child and hours and hours of his life — and would go on and on drudging, through thousands and thousands of pages, not one of them publishable, to the end of my life — so I suppose that what I've discovered at last is my — well, let's use the word. My talent. Perhaps it's been growing down there, in the dark, all this time — until finally it's strong enough to take over, eh? Anyway, now all I've got to do is a bit of pruning, no doubt some tightening up — correct the spelling and the typing mistakes, and float an extract or two in Nigel's currently fashionable little magazine — I've been promising him for years — (*He laughs.*)

QUARTERMAINE *enters through the French windows.*

QUARTERMAINE. All clear, then? Hello, Mark!

WINDSCAPE. What — oh good heavens, St. John — yes, yes, I forgot that you were still out there.

QUARTERMAINE. Oh no — I enjoyed it — to tell you the truth it seems to have cleared my head — I was feeling a bit — a bit odd before — Hello Mark!

SACKLING. Hello, St. John, have a good holiday?

QUARTERMAINE. Yes — yes — terrific thanks! Terrific! And how were they?

SACKLING. Who?

QUARTERMAINE. Camelia. And little Tom too. Weren't you going to see them over half term?

SACKLING. Oh, that's right. Actually, as it turned out, they were unavailable. Tom was getting over mumps, or so at least Camelia claimed, so she decided to take him to a friend of her mother's, in Wales, to convalesce. They have a cottage by the sea, and of course I couldn't offer him that, could I? Even though this half-term was mine, according to the agreement.

WINDSCAPE, *during this, goes to his briefcase, takes out books, puts them on top of the tape-recorder, puts his briefcase and other books in the locker, etc.*

QUARTERMAINE. Still, perhaps it did him some good — I mean, the beach and the valleys and hills and — and — I mean if poor little Tom's been ill —

SACKLING. St. John, I'd be grateful if you'd stop referring to him as little Tom, and *poor* little Tom too, it makes him sound like something out of the workhouse, and he's anyway not so little any more, the last time I saw him he must have weighed in at a good five stone —

QUARTERMAINE. What? Oh — oh right. (*A little pause.*) Five stone, eh? (*He whistles.*) Um — but what a pity I didn't know you were stuck in Cambridge over the half, we could have got together — but perhaps you got some writing done —

SACKLING. Yes — well some — as always —

ANITA *enters through the French windows.*

SACKLING. Hi, Anita!

QUARTERMAINE. Hello, Anita!

WINDSCAPE. Anita, my dear —

ANITA *takes off her coat. She is pregnant.*

SACKLING. — you're swelling along pleasantly. Rapidly too.

ANITA *laughs.*

QUARTERMAINE. But you look — you look — (*Gazing at her in a sort of reverence.*) I mean (*He gestures.*) in just a week, good Lord!

ANITA. Well, it's taken a bit longer than a week, St. John.

QUARTERMAINE. No, no, but I mean —

WINDSCAPE. Just like Fanny, nothing shows for ages and then one day there it is — for the world to see —

SACKLING. And how's Nigel getting on in New York?

ANITA. Oh, he decided not to go. He suddenly became convinced
— had a dream, or something — that I'd spawn prematurely, so
he stayed at home and mugged up on all the texts — Spock for
practicals, and Blake and D.H. Lawrence and some Indian
writer he's discovered and is going to publish, for significance
— which was lovely for me as I didn't have to go to my parents,
I spent most of the time in the bath reading thrillers. It was
lovely.

QUARTERMAINE. Oh, I wish I'd known you were here, so was
Mark, as it turned out, weren't you Mark, we could have got
together — but I say, it's good to be back in a way, isn't it — I
mean, after a good holiday of course —

SACKLING. Tell him I'm going to give him a ring, will you —
(*To* ANITA.)

The sound of the door opening, and closing, during this.

— there's something I've got for him. At last.

ANITA. Oh Mark, really! He'll be so thrilled — he keeps refusing
to 'phone you because he says it's like soliciting —

QUARTERMAINE. Hello, Derek, have you had a good half —?

MEADLE enters.

(*Laughing.*) But of course I've seen you already, I'm sorry if I
was a bit — off-colour, don't know what was the matter with
me — but oh Lord, what have you done to your cheek — I
didn't even notice it before, you do get in the wars, though,
don't you, old man. Was it shaving?

ANITA. Are you all right, Derek? You don't look —

MEADLE. Yes, yes thanks — well — (*He laughs.*) apart from just
finding out that I won't be joining you as a full-time member
of the staff. In fact, my hours are going to be cut. By over a
quarter. Which won't give me enough money to survive on.
Furthermore, unless there's a sudden swing upwards in
enrolment, I may not have any hours at all next month. So I'll
— I'll probably be leaving you then.

QUARTERMAINE. Leave! Oh no! That's rotten!

WINDSCAPE. I'm very sorry Dennis. I blame myself. I should have explained more fully. But you were out of the room so quickly —

SACKLING. Look, we must have a word with Thomas, with Eddie — we can't allow Derek just to be chucked out — Henry, perhaps you could speak to Eddie and Thomas on behalf of us all —

ANITA. Yes. Henry, you will, won't you?

WINDSCAPE. Of course I'll — I'll do my best. But you see the financial situation — it's not at all good, at the moment, is it? The school can only afford what it can afford. But whatever happens, Dennis — it's no reflection on your teaching. None at all.

MEADLE. Oh, I know that. It's Derek, by the way, Henry. (*Laughing.*) But that's life, isn't it? That's the joke. How hard I've worked. I mean, old Quartermaine here — well, according to one of the Swedes I'm not allowed to mention because it's a fraction on the unethical side to speak ill of a colleague — well, he sometimes sits for a whole hour not speaking. Even in dictation classes. Or if he does condescend to speak, goes off into little stories about himself they can't make head or tail of.

There is a pause.

QUARTERMAINE. What, a Swede, did you say? What does he look like?

MEADLE. Oh, what does it matter? Everybody knows that for you one Swede is like another German, one Greek is like another Italian, you can't tell them apart and you don't know what they're called — unlike me, you see — because do you know what I do? I memorize their names before their first class, and then study their faces during it, and then when I go home I close my eyes and practise putting the two together so that by the second class I know every one of my students *personally,* and do you know what else I do, I keep a look-out not only in term-time but also in my holidays — my *unpaid* holidays — for any item that might interest them for British Life and Institutions and actually make a note of them — here

— in my notebook, which I always keep especially in my pocket (*Wrestling with it with increasing violence, jerking it out of his pocket, tearing his pocket as he does so.*) along with any of the out-of-the-way idioms and interesting usages I might happen across — and do you know what *else* I do — I — but what does it matter what else I do, that's what I mean by joke or life or whatever it is, because I'm the one that's facing the push, and you're the one that's on permanent. (*During this speech* MEADLE's *accent has become increasingly North Country.*) Not that I begrudge you — it's just that I reckon that I've earned it. Look — look, I don't mean — I don't mean — the last thing I mean is — (*He turns away, possibly in tears.*)

There is silence, into which MELANIE *enters, through the French windows.*

QUARTERMAINE. Oh hello, Melanie, have a good half?

WINDSCAPE. Hello Melanie, my dear.

SACKLING. Melanie.

ANITA. Hello Melanie.

MELANIE *goes to the table, puts down her briefcase, takes off her coat.*

QUARTERMAINE. Um — um — how's your mother?

WINDSCAPE. Yes, how — how is she?

MELANIE. She's dead. She died last Tuesday.

There is silence.

WINDSCAPE. Oh Melanie — I'm so sorry — so sorry —

Murmurings from the others.

Was it another attack, my dear?

MELANIE. No. she fell down the stairs and broke her neck. We don't quite know how it happened as it was after I'd gone to bed. Nurse Grimes found her there in the morning, I still hadn't got up, the first I knew of it was Nurse Grimes calling me — and — and — that's really all there is to tell. I'd be grateful if we could dispense with condolences and that sort of thing, because what I really want most of all is to get on in the usual fashion, without any — any fuss. I shall tell Thomas and Eddie, naturally, straight away —

The sound of the door opening: footsteps, rather odd, though.

LOOMIS. Hello everybody, hello, all rested up I trust, welcome back, welcome back — but first, is Melanie here, ah there you are, Melanie my dear. (*Appearing on stage. He has a stick, his glasses are tinted, and his voice and manner are frailer.*) There are a couple of policemen in the office with Thomas, who want a word with you. They refuse to say what about, but not to worry, not to worry, because I asked whether it was illness or accident, and they assured me it wasn't, so your mother's perfectly all right, my dear, which is the main thing, isn't it, it's probably some nonsense to do with your car, anyway if you'd go along to the office and flirt with them — and whatever you do, don't let Thomas lose his temper. (*He laughs.*)

MELANIE *stands for a moment, then braces herself and walks off, left, as:*

Really! our Cambridge bobbies, they always have to make such a solemn meal out of the most trivial business — pursuing their enquiries on information received, as they put it — goodness knows how they'd behave if they had something truly serious — Anita, my dear, how blooming you look, how blooming — and how did Nigel find New York?

ANITA. Oh fine, thank you Eddie, fine —

LOOMIS. Good good good, well tell Nigel how much we're looking forward to the first Anglo-American edition, and how sorry we are we've had to cut back to just the one subscription but *semper fidelis*. Henry what sort of half term did you have — one of your adventurous caravan treks, where to this time?

WINDSCAPE. Yes Eddie — to Norfolk.

LOOMIS. Weather all right, I trust?

WINDSCAPE. Oh yes, Eddie, yes, lovely thank you, except when it rained and — and even then we had one — one amazing moment at sunrise —

LOOMIS. Good, good, especially for Fanny, little Fanny, Ben and Susan eh — and how did Susan get on with her 'O' levels, results as expected?

WINDSCAPE. Yes, Eddie, thanks, lots of — of Bs and — and — Cs and — and so forth.

LOOMIS. I'm not surprised, with you and Fanny behind her, give her our congratulations do, and Mark — if that is Mark I see behind a week's further fuzzy-wuzzy, lots of tap, tap, tapping?

SACKLING. Oh, well, yes — yes, a little, thanks Eddie.

LOOMIS. Well keep at it, we know that one day — ah, there's our Derek, but I've already said my welcomes to him, haven't I Derek, in the corridor — I gather you found Thomas?

MEADLE. Yes thank you, Eddie, yes yes.

LOOMIS. And that you got whatever it was you were so anxious to get sorted out, sorted out, at least Thomas seemed very pleased with the fruits of your deliberations.

MEADLE. Well — well yes, thank you, Eddie, all sorted out, yes.

LOOMIS. Good, good — and St. John, now what was I going to say to you — oh, I remember — in spite of this tired old brain of mine — yet another post-card for you in the office, from that fervent fan your Swiss, I hope you don't mind my having a peek, but I always think post-cards — what's his name?

QUARTERMAINE. Um, Muller isn't it —

LOOMIS. Boller, I think it is. Ferdinand Boller. How lucky that you don't have to recall his name to his face, or he might not go on being so devoted to you, anyway, he's hoping to see you when he's in England on business late this year, or next or some time or never, that is, if I understand him correctly, his English actually seems to get worse from post-card to post-card, though we can't hold you responsible for that, can we, at this stage — (*He laughs.*) now, now there's something I'd like to take the opportunity of saying to you, just between ourselves, and a little behind Thomas's back, so to speak, I expect you've all noticed the very distinct drop in student enrolment these last few months. Thomas is slightly more worried than perhaps he's let any of you realise, we all know how dedicated he is to the future of the school — and to the future of the staff —

QUARTERMAINE. Hear, hear!

LOOMIS. — we've long thought of you as part of a family, I think you all know that we do our best to care for you in that spirit —

QUARTERMAINE. Absolutely!

LOOMIS. — and I'm sure you're all wondering what you can do to help us through this little rough patch — and the answer is, to go on giving of your very best to your teaching, and to show what students we've got that while we may not be as grand as some schools in Cambridge, we yield to no school in the country in the thing that matters most, our devotion to their devotion to their learning of our language.

QUARTERMAINE (*amid murmurs*). Hear, hear!

LOOMIS. That's how we can best serve our school at this time of slight crisis, and as I say, this is strictly *entre nous*, without reference to Thomas. Thank you everybody and bless you all — the bell will ring in a minute or so I believe, so — (*He gestures.*)

And as all except QUARTERMAINE *move to their lockers, etc:*

QUARTERMAINE. Eddie that was — that was terrific!

LOOMIS. St. John a word of warning, I'm afraid there have been a number of complaints about your teaching — Thomas, I regret to say, received a round robin before half-term.

QUARTERMAINE. Oh Lord, that Swede, you mean?

LOOMIS. What Swede?

During this, the sound of the door opening: footsteps.

Ah — Melanie, my dear, you've cleared it up, have you, what

was it all about?

MELANIE. Oh yes, Eddie. All too preposterous. Apparently a group of French girls — from my intermediary Life and Institutions got hold of the wrong end of the stick. They didn't realize my recipe for roasting swan was for a medieval banquet, and actually tried to kill one on the Cam, can you believe it! Club one to death from a punt, with the intention of taking it back to their rooms and cooking and eating it! And then when they were reported to the police, blamed me. I'm glad to say that the swan, being a swan, survived. And gave one of them a badly bruised arm. Typically French. (*She goes to her locker.*)

Amidst laughter from all except WINDSCAPE *the bell rings. They all move towards the door, with books, etc, except for* QUARTERMAINE, *who goes to his locker, stands before it looking puzzled, takes out one or two books, slightly confused.*

QUARTERMAINE. If it's not dictation it must be comprehension. Or — or — oh Lord!

Lights.

Scene Two

A Friday evening, some months later. The French windows are open. QUARTERMAINE *is asleep in an armchair, papers and books on his lap. He is visible to the audience, but not to anyone on stage who doesn't look specifically in the armchair.*
     QUARTERMAINE *suddenly groans. There is a pause.*

QUARTERMAINE (*in his sleep*). Oh Lord ! (*A pause.*) I say! (*A pause. He laughs, sleeps.*)

The sound of the door opening: footsteps.

MELANIE *enters from the left. She goes to her locker, puts her books in.*

QUARTERMAINE, *not heard, or perhaps half heard, by*

MELANIE, *lets out a groan.*

MELANIE *takes an over-night bag out of her locker.*

QUARTERMAINE (*lets out another groan, rises to his feet*). Oh, Lord!

MELANIE (*starts, turns, sees* QUARTERMAINE). St. John! (*She goes towards him.*) Are you all right?

QUARTERMAINE (*blinks at her*). Oh — oh yes thanks — um — Melanie — next class, is it?

MELANIE. Heavens no, we've finished for the day. For the week, in fact.

QUARTERMAINE (*clearly confused*). Oh, I — I didn't hear the bell.

MELANIE. It hasn't gone yet. Don't worry, Eddie's having one of his very out-of-sorts days, poor lamb, and Thomas is in the office. We're safe.

QUARTERMAINE. Oh. Oh yes — I suppose I must have let them go early — always restless on a Friday, aren't they, and then sat down and — and —

MELANIE. St. John, what are you doing tonight?

QUARTERMAINE. Oh — usual — nothing very —

MELANIE. Then I'd like to introduce you to some very special friends of mine. Would you like that?

QUARTERMAINE. Well yes — yes — thank you, Melanie.

MELANIE. I'm sure you'll enjoy it — we always end up with singing and dancing, the food's delicious and the people are — well you'll see for yourself.

QUARTERMAINE. Well, it sounds — sounds terrific!

The sound of the door: footsteps.

MELANIE. Right, you wait for me here, and I'll come and collect you when I'm ready — Oh hello Derek, you too — what a bunch of skyvers we're all turning out to be, eh?

MEADLE. Yes, well, it's only a few minutes off — besides Daphne's coming down for the weekend, I don't want to miss her train —

MELANIE (*going out*). Jolly good — give her my love —

MEADLE. Right, Melanie, right — but I had a bloody near one in the corridor I can tell you. I was sloping past the office — terrible din coming from it, sounded like a gang of Germans, all bellowing away and Thomas trying to calm them down — anyway I'd just got past the door when Eddie came round the corner.

QUARTERMAINE. Phew!

MEADLE. Yes. I began to mumble some nonsense about wanting to check up on a student — you know — but thinking I'd better wait until Thomas was freer — but he didn't see me — went right on past — I mean, we were like that! (*Showing.*)

QUARTERMAINE. Oh Lord! (*Laughing.*) Still, I hope he's all right — I mean for him not to notice —

MEADLE. Oh, by the way, I've got an invitation for you. You know Daphne and I are engaged — not that we haven't been from the moment I walked into the library and saw her again. But now that I've got my permanency, we might as well make it official. We'll get married on the first day of the summer vac, and I'm going to ask Thomas and Eddie to be best man. I mean, let them decide which — I don't want to upset one by choosing the other.

QUARTERMAINE. Congratulations! Terrific! And then off on your honey-moon, eh?

MEADLE. Yes. We've settled for Hayling Island. Not very exciting, I know, but there may be a way to pick up a little money as well as having a good holiday ourselves. Daphne's keen to start saving for a house — you know how it is, there's a very practical head on those little shoulders of hers. There's a good chance she might even come and do a bit of teaching here — to replace me as the part-time, you see. I've already dropped a little hint to Thomas — I think he was worried by her speech impediment, but I pointed out that in some respects that could be an asset — with the elementary groups, for instance, and especially the Japs — that she understands the problems of pronunciation from inside, so to speak.

QUARTERMAINE. Absolutely — and she'd be — a great asset here, wouldn't she, in the staff-room, I mean — she's a wonderful girl, Derek.

MEADLE. Yes, well, I think you'll like her even more when you meet her. Because frankly she's — she's — (*He shakes his head.*) And I'll tell you something — I don't know whether you've noticed but since she came back I've stopped having all those ridiculous accidents. They were the bane of my life, even though I was always trying to make light of them. I suppose it's — it's something to do with needing — well, well, the right person, eh? Love. Let's face it. Love. Oh, I'd better get going. So see you at seven. It'll be nothing special, but my landlady wants to put on a celebration supper — she's already very fond of Daphne, by the way — and she said if I wanted to ask along a friend — and there's nobody I'd rather have —

QUARTERMAINE. Derek, I'm very — I'm very honoured —

MEADLE. Actually, you'd better make it 6.30, as it'll be more on the lines of a high tea. And if you could bring along a couple of bottles of wine —

QUARTERMAINE. My dear chap, I'll bring — I'll bring *champagne* — and — and — oh Lord, I'd forgotten! Oh no! I've already accepted an invitation for this evening.

MEADLE. Oh. What to?

QUARTERMAINE. Well, I can't make out, quite — I was in a bit of a haze when Melanie asked me, but she said something about friends and singing and dancing —

MEADLE. And you accepted?

QUARTERMAINE. Well yes. She seemed so — so anxious — and anyway —

MEADLE. But it's — it's — one of those evenings. What they sing is hymns and dancing is up and down and around and about and then that Nurse Grimes declares for Jesus — and then the rest of them follow suit, and then they all stand around and

wait for you to do it — at least, that's how it went the night
she got me along. She's trying to convert you.

QUARTERMAINE. Oh Lord — oh Lord —

The bell rings.

MEADLE. But I told you all about it —

QUARTERMAINE. Yes, but I'd forgotten — I mean she didn't
mention Jesus —

MEADLE. Well, she won't let you get out of it now. (*During this,
he has been getting ready to go, putting on his bicycle clips,
etc.*)

*Off, from the garden, foreign voices, laughing, calling out, etc,
some of them Japanese; among them* SACKLING's, *calling out
goodnights, in the distance. Then:*

SACKLING (*closer*). No, sorry, I really can't — I'm in a hurry —
and anyway — most of the mallets are broken and there aren't
enough balls — so goodnight — goodnight —

SACKLING *enters, as* MEADLE *speaks.*

MEADLE. Well, I'll get you and Daphne together very soon —
don't worry — (*Making to go.*) Here, Mark, guess what
St. John's got himself into — one of Melanie's evenings.

SACKLING (*in a hurry, with books etc*). Christ, you haven't, have
you? (*He is clean-shaven, by the way.*) You *are* a chump,
St. John, you must have heard her going on about her dark
night of the soul, after her mother died, and how Nurse Grimes
introduced her to her sect and redeemed her — she's talked
about nothing else for months and — and anyway I remember
telling you how she tried it on me — don't you take anything
in!

QUARTERMAINE. Yes, yes I did, but — but —

SACKLING. But you didn't know how to say no. Which, if I may
say so, is both your charm and your major weakness.

QUARTERMAINE. Well, you never know — it may be — may be
quite interesting — one has to — has to have a go at anything
really — and I wasn't doing anything else this evening.

SACKLING (*who is now ready to go*). This evening! Yes, you
bloody *are* doing something else this evening. You're going out
to dinner.

QUARTERMAINE. What — where?

SACKLING. At my place — oh Christ! Don't say I forgot to
invite you. Well you're invited. So there you are, saved from
salvation. All you have to do is to tell Melanie that you'd
forgotten —

QUARTERMAINE. Oh, this is terrible. You mean I'd be having
dinner with you?

SACKLING. You *are* having dinner with us. It's obligatory. For
one thing, I told Camelia I'd asked you — she's counting on
you — we all are — even Tom, I promised him he could stay
up an extra half-an-hour to see you again — you're always
going on about looking forward to seeing him — (*He is putting
on bicycle clips. The first time in the play.*)

QUARTERMAINE. But what about Melanie? I promised her —

SACKLING. Oh, to hell with Melanie! It's all a load of pathetic
nonsense — and probably blasphemous, too, if one believed in
God. Look, speaking as one of your best and oldest and dearest
etc — it's *crucial* that you come. Of the greatest importance.
To me. You see. OK? Look, I've got to dash, I'm picking Tom
up from school —

The sound of the door opening: footsteps.

Make sure (*To off.*) that he turns up tonight, won't you? He's
got himself into one of his usual messes — see you both at
eight. (*He goes as:*)

*ANITA enters. She has a look of weariness about her, is subtly
less well-turned out than in previous scenes.*

QUARTERMAINE. Oh don't say you and Nigel are going to be
there too — oh — oh —

ANITA. Why can't you come?

QUARTERMAINE. Well I fell into one of those dozes again —
you know how they keep coming over me suddenly — for a
minute or so — and — and when I came out of it, there I was,

right in the middle of this — this Melanie business.

ANITA. Poor St. John.

QUARTERMAINE. But I can't just turn round to her now — she
  was so — well her eyes — I can't explain — very — well —
  and anyway I can't just turn round now and say sorry Melanie,
  something much better's turned up — oh, if only Mark hadn't
  forgotten! — but I suppose he knows I'm usually free — and —
  thought he had — or — but what do I do, Anita, Mark seems
  so — so determined, too. What do I do?

ANITA. I don't know. But come if you can. It's meant to be a
  reconciliation dinner, and you know how they usually turn
  out. So you'd be a great help, as the perfect outsider.

QUARTERMAINE. Well, you know I'd do anything — anything —
  to make sure that old Mark and his Camelia and little Tom too,
  of course, stay together.

ANITA. Oh, it's not them that need reconciling. They already are.

QUARTERMAINE. Oh.

ANITA. It's Mark and Nigel. Hasn't Mark told you anything
  about that?

QUARTERMAINE. No. Nothing. You mean old Mark and old
  Nigel — oh, Lord, but they're such friends, what happened?

ANITA. Oh, it was all a couple of months ago. They had the most
  appalling row, because Nigel turned down an extract from
  Mark's novel. About seven extracts, actually.

SACKLING. Oh no. Oh, poor Mark!

ANITA. Well, Nigel made everything worse by deciding to be
  completely honest for once. I suppose he thought Mark, being
  an old friend, had it coming to him. What he said was that
  everything Mark had sent him was imitative and laboured, and
  anyway who really cared any more about the mysteries of sex,
  the wonders of childbirth, the delicacies of personal
  relationships — it had all been done and done and done to
  death, there were far bigger issues.

QUARTERMAINE. Oh Lord, oh Lord! Are there?

ANITA. So of course when the magazine folded, and Nigel was
    going through his rough patch, with the printers threatening to
    sue and various other things, Mark wrote him a gloating letter
    saying how delighted he was as *Reports* had never been
    interested in serious literary values, only in pandering to the
    top names — or trying to — and added a PS about the old
    Amanda Southgate affair, claiming to be indignant on my
    account, I must say, I rather wish he'd resisted that.

QUARTERMAINE. But still — but still — he has asked Nigel to
    dinner —

ANITA. Oh, that was probably Camelia. She never took literature
    seriously, and now that Mark's sworn off writing — at least for
    the time — the important thing for her is that we had them to
    dinner just before she left Mark, and now she's come back
    she's realised she owes us the return. I loathe the thought of it
    — for one thing we haven't been able to find a baby-sitter, so
    we'll have to bring Ophelia in her carry-cot — she's still got
    six weeks colic, after four months — so it would be nice if you
    came, St. John, you'd make the whole thing more bearable.

QUARTERMAINE. Oh, I'd love to — and to see Ophelia — I've
    only seen her the once, in hospital — what hair she had!

    ANITA *laughs. Is in fact crying slightly.*

    Oh Anita — what is it — oh, Lord, I hate to see you unhappy —
    more than anyone else — (*He makes a move towards her,
    checks himself, makes a move again.*) Oh Lord! (*He stands
    before her, helplessly.*)

ANITA. I'm all right, St. John, honestly — it's just that — oh, the
    way things go, I mean. Or don't go. Nothing seems to come out
    right. All the years I adored him and he couldn't bear me. And
    now he adores me and I can't bear him. You see. (*She looks at
    him.*) What a — what a nice man you are. (*She begins to cry
    again.*) I'm tired, I expect, tired — (*Turning away, blowing her
    nose, wiping her eyes, etc, as:*)

    The sound of the door opening: footsteps.

QUARTERMAINE (*turning*). Oh — oh hello Henry, you've finished
    finished late — um —

WINDSCAPE (*appearing rather heavily*). Yes, I got into a bit of a tangle with my Intermediary British Life and Institutions, over our parliamentary system. Usually it's perfectly clear to me but this time it all came out rather oddly. Or it must have done, as I had the whole lot of them dismissing it with contempt — the three or four from the Eastern bloc, all the ones from Fascist countries, the Spanish, the Portuguese, the South Americans — the French were the loudest, as always — but even the Japanese — normally such a polite, reticent man — and I don't see quite how it happened or what I said, but it was rather hard being lectured at on — on political decencies — and shouted at by — by — still, I suppose it's better they should all join up for a wrangle with me than with each other — although to tell you the truth I found it rather hard to keep my temper (*Sitting down.*) but I think I managed to — with the result that I've got a — a slight headache. After all, I was only *explaining* our constitution, not boasting about it. I've got my own — own distinct reservations — no system's perfect, as I kept having to say to Santos. His father's a Bolivian cabinet minister.

ANITA (*who has been discreetly composing herself during the above*). It's awful when they get like that, isn't it? I always make them explain our politics to me, and then just correct their English, whatever they say — one of the advantages of being female, I suppose — (*She attempts a little laugh.*) well, goodnight, Henry, see you Monday —

WINDSCAPE. 'Night, Anita, my dear. Best to Nigel, and little Ophelia —

ANITA. And St. John, see you later I hope. Do, if you can.

QUARTERMAINE. Yes, well — I'll — I'll — right, Anita. Right. If I can.

ANITA *goes out through the French windows.*

There is a pause. WINDSCAPE *is sitting in the chair, stroking his forehead.*

QUARTERMAINE (*is standing in a state of desperation*). I say, Henry — I say — I wonder if you could give me some advice.

WINDSCAPE. Mmmm?

QUARTERMAINE. I'm in a bit of a pickle, you see.

WINDSCAPE. Oh. Oh good heavens, St. John, that reminds me —
I'd completely forgotten — is there any chance you could
come over tonight?

QUARTERMAINE. What?

WINDSCAPE. I'm sorry it's such short notice, it wouldn't have
been if I'd remembered. The thing is that Fanny's really very
down in the dumps, very down, she really does need an
evening out. So do I, come to that. It's Susan, you see. She's
taken a turn for the worse.

QUARTERMAINE. Oh — oh —

WINDSCAPE. Oh, it's probably just withdrawal from all the
tranquillising drugs they put her on, in hospital, and then her
friends would keep coming over in the evenings and talking
about their plans and their blasted 'A' levels and of course
there's no possibility that Susan — at least for a few years —
anyway, last night, she laughed at something on television, a
good sign, Fanny and I thought, the first time she's laughed
since her breakdown, so we didn't realise until we were in the
living-room that what we were laughing at was a news flash to
do with some particularly hideous atrocity in — in — (*He
gestures.*) and what followed was a bit of a nightmare,
especially for Ben and little Fanny — it ended with the doctor
having to sedate her — almost forcibly, I'm afraid — so — so I
noticed La Règle du Jeu at the Arts, one of our favourite
films, so decent and — and humane — and then a quiet dinner
afterwards at the French place — just the two of us — if you
could manage it. You're the only person Susan will allow to
baby-sit, you see. She seems to feel some — some reassurance
from you. And of course little Fanny and Benjamin love it too,
when you come.

QUARTERMAINE. I'd love to, Henry — love to — but could it be
Saturday?

WINDSCAPE. No, Saturday's no good — we have our family
therapy session in the afternoon and we all feel so — so
exhausted afterwards. Demoralised, really. I've still to be

persuaded that they serve a — a useful — though of course one mustn't prejudge —

QUARTERMAINE. Sunday, then?

WINDSCAPE. Unfortunately Fanny's mother's coming on Sunday. Rather against our inclinations as — as she's rather insensitive with Susan — advises her to pull her socks up — that sort of thing — you can't manage this evening then.

QUARTERMAINE. Well, I — I — you see the problem is — I can't —

The sound of the door opening: footsteps. MELANIE appears. She has changed her dress, is wearing high-heeled shoes, some make-up, and has taken much trouble with her hair.

MELANIE. Well, there we are then, St. John — sorry to have been so long — oh, hello, Henry, I didn't know you were still here.

WINDSCAPE. Hello Melanie (*Slightly awkward.*) Oh, I've been meaning to say all day how much I like that dress.

MELANIE (*smiles*). Thank you. I'm taking St. John to one of my evenings —

WINDSCAPE. Oh. Oh yes. I'm so sorry that Fanny and I have been unable to come so far —

MELANIE. Oh, I know how difficult things are for you at the moment — as long as you both realise that any time you want to come along, I've been thinking that perhaps Susan might —

WINDSCAPE. Yes, yes, thank you, Melanie. (*Cutting her slightly.*)

MELANIE. Are you all right, you look a little fraught.

WINDSCAPE. Oh just tired, Friday eveningish, that's all.

QUARTERMAINE. And a bit of a headache — eh Henry?

MELANIE. Oh? Where?

WINDSCAPE. Well — in my head.

MELANIE. Yes, but which part?

WINDSCAPE. Well, it seems to be — just here — (*Rubbing his brow.*)

MELANIE. Ah, well then it's a tension headache, Nurse Grimes showed me a marvellous trick for dealing with that, let me have a go at it. (*She comes over to* WINDSCAPE, *behind the chair.*) Now put your head forward — right forward —

WINDSCAPE *does so, with perceptible lack of enthusiasm.*

MELANIE. There. Now. (*She proceeds to knead her fingers into the back of* WINDSCAPE'*s neck.*)

QUARTERMAINE. So that's how they do it — looks jolly relaxing, anyway —

WINDSCAPE *endures for a few seconds, then suddenly lets out a cry, leaps up.*

There is a pause.

WINDSCAPE. I'm — Melanie, I'm sorry — I — don't know quite what —

MELANIE. I expect I hurt you, pressed the wrong nerve or — I still haven't quite got the trick of it, with my clumsy —

WINDSCAPE. Well — well actually it feels a little better. (*He tries a laugh.*) Thank you.

MELANIE (*smiles*). Well, St. John, we'd better be on our way. It's quite a drive. Goodnight, Henry, and rest yourself during the weekend, won't you?

WINDSCAPE. Yes, yes — the same to you (*A slight hesitation.*) my dear. Goodnight, St. John, see you Monday.

QUARTERMAINE. See you Monday Henry and — oh, if it turns out that Saturday or Sunday — well, I'm sure I'll be free —

WINDSCAPE *smiles, nods.*

As they go out through the French windows there is the sound of the door opening and feet, a stick.

WINDSCAPE. Oh hello Eddie, I didn't know you were about today.

LOOMIS (*enters. He is much frailer than when last seen*). Well, there was a frightful schmozzle in the office — and Henry asked me to come down — but was that St. John's voice I heard just now?

WINDSCAPE. Yes. His and Melanie's —

LOOMIS. Ah. Well, I would have quite liked a word with our St. John. He's caused us quite an afternoon. He appears to have missed his last class entirely. His students waited doggedly through the whole hour for him to turn up, and then went to the office and berated poor Thomas — they were mostly Germans, and you know what they're like if they think they're not getting their money's worth of syllabus.

WINDSCAPE. Oh dear.

LOOMIS. Though I doubt whether they'd get much more sensible English from St. John present than from St. John absent — as far as I know that Swiss Ferdinand Boller is the only student who ever felt he got value for money from St. John, thank goodness he's stopped sending those post-cards at last, they made Thomas quite upset — but I wonder what it was he enjoyed so much about St. John's classes — perhaps the lack of — of — I don't know what we're going to do about him in the end, though, if we turned him out where would he go, who else would have him, one does look after one's own, I suppose, when it comes to it I agree with Thomas on that, after all the school's our — our family, the only family Thomas and I have between us, so one has a responsibility for them — but a responsibility for the students too — (*There should be a slightly rambling quality in the delivery of this speech.*) it's so difficult to get the balance right — so difficult — St. John forgetting to teach them, and now Melanie's starting up her missionary work amongst them,— Thomas is going to have a word with her too — the Catholic countries won't stand for it, and why should they, and now our Meadle, taking to slipping away before the bell now he's got his permanency, trying to bluff his way past me in the hall as if I couldn't see him — ha — well, at least Mark's pulling his weight now he's got his Camelia back, I never thought for a moment there was a writer in that lad, did you? — and Anita — really I don't know how these modern young couples cope — but I gather Nigel's taken to it wonderfully, Thomas and I saw the three of them on the Backs the other day, a very pretty sight it was too — so — so — good, good, — just the problems of a flourishing school, eh? (*He laughs.*)

WINDSCAPE. Yes. Yes indeed, Eddie.

LOOMIS. Well, I'd best get back up to bed, or Thomas will have a fit, goodnight Henry, see you Monday, bless you, bless you.

WINDSCAPE. Yes, see you Monday Eddie.

LOOMIS (*goes off, stops*). Oh, I haven't asked for a while — how's our Susan?

WINDSCAPE. Oh I think responding — slowly — slowly responding.

LOOMIS. Good, good. (*The sound of the door closing.*)

During this, the sound of students' voices, young, distant, in the garden. They get closer as the scene concludes.

WINDSCAPE *stands for a moment, touches his forehead, then goes to his locker, puts away his books, gets his briefcase.*

The sound of student's voices, probably two girls, two boys, now laughing, calling out to each other in some sort of game.

WINDSCAPE *gets out his bicycle clips, bends to put them on. As he does so he looks towards the French windows, smiles slightly, continues putting on the clips, as the sound of voices, still raised in laughter, continues.*

Curtain.

Scene Three

Eighteen months later. It is around Christmas. Not yet dark, but darkening slightly. The French windows are closed, but the curtains are open. There is an atmosphere of chill. One table-light is on.

SACKLING, QUARTERMAINE, MELANIE, ANITA, WINDSCAPE *and* MEADLE *are variously sitting and standing.*

SACKLING *is smoking a pipe. He has a beard.* WINDSCAPE *is also smoking a pipe.* ANITA *is pregnant.* MEADLE *has a plaster neck-brace.* QUARTERMAINE *is wearing a dinner-jacket.*

MELANIE *is sitting, rather hunched, nervously smoking a cigarette. It is the first time in the play that she has smoked. She smokes throughout the scene, lighting one after another.*

After a pause.

SACKLING. It's always at Christmas, somehow, isn't it?

WINDSCAPE. Yes.

SACKLING. Oh Henry, I'm sorry —

WINDSCAPE. No. you're right. I was thinking much the same thing, Both my parents too, but — but of course in Susan's case I don't think the season was — was relevant. At least to her. The blinds were always down, you see. Because any brightness hurt her mind. Natural brightness, that is. She could tolerate artificial light. Until the last — last bit.

ANITA (*there is a faint touch of querulousness in her voice*). Look. I'm sorry, but I'll have to go soon, I'm afraid. I promised the *au pair* she could have the night off, and Nigel's probably not coming back from London until tomorrow —

MEADLE. Yes, I've got to get back pretty soon. Daphne's not too grand, what with her morning sickness and all the redecorating — she's been over-doing it and I promised — I don't want to leave her alone too long.

WINDSCAPE. Of course — of course — there's really no need for all of us when it comes to it — it's just that — that — as soon as I heard I had some idea that you would want — well — without perhaps enough consideration — it was a bad idea, perhaps —

QUARTERMAINE. Oh, I say Henry — well, I'm jolly glad you got in touch with me — though of course I wasn't doing anything in particular —

SACKLING. Well, I must say, St. John, (*Smiling.*) you do look as if you might have been about to be up to something —

QUARTERMAINE. What? Oh — (*He laughs.*) well, no, no, not

really — it was just — just —

During this, the sound of the door opening. They all look towards it: the sound of footsteps, dragging feet, a stick.

LOOMIS (*in an over-coat, with a stick, and with a deaf-aid attached to his glasses*). I saw the lights on so I guessed that some of you — one or two perhaps — had come. But I didn't expect all of you. Not at this time of year, with your families and responsibilities. Thomas would have been so touched. So touched. My thanks on his behalf. My thanks. (*A little pause*.) He died an hour ago. They did everything they could, right to the end, but of course, as we've all known for some time, there was nothing to be done. (*A little pause*.) You know how much you all meant to him. He talked of every one of you, every evening, until — (*He gestures*.) But you'll also want to know what its future is to be, this school that he loved so much. I know what his wishes are, we discussed them quite openly once we both knew that he was bound to leave us. I've also talked to Henry. I'm sure it will be no surprise to all of you that I asked Henry some time ago to take over the school as its sole Principal. I've no desire to take an active part in it, now that Thomas is no longer here. I loved it for his sake, you see. I'll make no secret of that. Not this evening. (*A pause, nearly breaks down, pulls himself together*.) Not this evening. I shall be leaving the flat as soon as possible — it has too many memories — and settle somewhere by the sea. As we'd always hoped to do. I hope that some of you will come and see me — (*A little pause*.) Bless you. Bless you. (*He turns and goes. The sound of his feet dragging slowly. The sound of the door shutting*.)

There is a pause.

WINDSCAPE. I — I really don't want to speak at such a moment about plans or changes. We'll have a meeting at the beginning of term to go into those, but I should just say that I've already talked to Mark, — at Eddie's suggestion and with Thomas's approval — a few weeks ago, when it became clear that Thomas was more than seriously ill — about his following me as the academic tutor. I am happy to say that he has accepted.

There are murmurs.

So until next term — which has a very reasonable enrolment, I am glad to report, let me merely assure you that I intend to do my best, as I know you will, to maintain our reputation as a — a flourishing school. I know — I know — Thomas and Eddie wouldn't want me to let you part without wishing you all a Happy Christmas.

Murmurs of 'Happy Christmas'.

Well, see you all next term!

They rise to go, putting on coats, etc.

QUARTERMAINE (*comes over to* WINDSCAPE). Henry — I say, well you and Mark — that's quite a team, you know.

WINDSCAPE. Thank you, St. John — I wonder if you could hang on a minute or so.

QUARTERMAINE. Absolutely. Oh absolutely, Henry.

SACKLING (*coated*). Well, night Henry — we'll speak. And St. John — over the Christmas, eh? You must come round. (*Gesturing with his pipe.*)

WINDSCAPE. Yes, we'll speak, Mark.

QUARTERMAINE. Oh, I'd love that — thanks Mark. See you then. Love to Camelia and Tom and little Mark too.

ANITA (*also coated*). Sorry if I was a little edgy earlier Henry. Put it down to my current condition and Yugoslav au pairs! (*She laughs.*)

WINDSCAPE. You get home to your Ophelia, my dear, and make Nigel look after you.

ANITA. Oh, I will, Henry — see you over Christmas, St. John, I hope.

QUARTERMAINE. Oh Lord yes — lovely — lovely — 'night, Anita.

MEADLE (*coated*). Sorry Daphne couldn't make it, Henry. She wanted to, of course. But I'll fill her in, don't worry, she's very much looking forward to her courses next term —

WINDSCAPE. And I'm looking forward to having her join us. Goodnight, Derek.

MEADLE. Drop around when you feel in the mood, St. John. Lots of paint-brushes for you to wield — (*He laughs.*)

QUARTERMAINE. Terrific! I love the smell of paint — love to Daphne —

MELANIE (*comes up, hunched, smoking*). 'Night Henry. 'Night.

WINDSCAPE. Night Melanie my dear. And perhaps we can all get together after Christmas — Fanny was saying how much she'd like to see you, after all this time.

MELANIE. Love to, love to, and St. John, if you're free pop around and have a drink. (*She laughs.*)

QUARTERMAINE. Oh yes please Melanie — I'd like that —

As SACKLING, ANITA, MEADLE, *and* MELANIE *leave, one after the other, the sound of their feet, and of the door opening and closing.*

QUARTERMAINE *and* WINDSCAPE *are left alone on stage.*

WINDSCAPE. Well, St. John — (*He hesitates.*) Where were you off to, tonight, by the way?

QUARTERMAINE. Oh Lord, nowhere Henry. (*He laughs.*) You see, there was a suitcase I still hadn't unpacked — it's been down in Mrs Harris' cellar all these years. But suddenly she wanted the space, so she made me take it up, and of course I opened it and there was this, (*Indicating the dinner-jacket.*) So I decided to try it on, to see if it still fits. And then you 'phoned, and Mrs Harris was doing her usual thing right beside me, glowering away (*He laughs.*) so — so I came straight on out here, forgetting I had it on. Stinks of moth-balls, I'm afraid, but not a bad fit, eh? Might come in useful sometime. But I say, poor old Eddie, poor old Eddie. Wasn't he — wasn't he terrific!

WINDSCAPE. Yes. Indeed. (*A slight pause.*) St. John. St. John. I've been worrying about this for — oh, ever since I realised I

was to take over from Eddie and Thomas. If I'm to be
principal, I have to run the school in my own way, you see.

QUARTERMAINE. Oh, I know that, Henry. We all do.

WINDSCAPE. And — and — I don't see, you see — however
fond of you I happen to be — we all happen to be — that
there's — there's any room for you anymore. You see?

QUARTERMAINE *nods.*

I thought it only right to tell you at the first — the very first
possible moment. So that you can — well, look around —

QUARTERMAINE. No, that's — right, thank you Henry. I — oh
Lord, I know that I haven't got much to offer — never had, I
suppose — and recently it's got even worse — it's a wonder —
a wonder people have put up with me so long, eh? (*He
attempts a laugh.*)

WINDSCAPE. If I could see any way —

QUARTERMAINE. No, no — I mean, it's no good being all right
in the staff-room if you're no good in the class-room, is it?
They're different things.

WINDSCAPE. I can't tell you how much I'll miss you. We all will.

QUARTERMAINE. And I — I'll miss it. All of you.

WINDSCAPE. Yes, I know. Would you like a quick drink — or —
or — come back and see Fanny.

QUARTERMAINE. Oh, no — no thank you Henry, I'll stay here
for a while — you know — and get myself used to — used to —
and — I'll go in a minute.

WINDSCAPE (*hesitates, looks at* QUARTERMAINE). Well,
goodnight, St. John.

QUARTERMAINE. Goodnight, Henry, see you next — (*He
gestures.*)

WINDSCAPE *goes off. The sound of feet and the door opening
and closing.*

QUARTERMAINE. Oh Lord! (*He walks a few steps, stops, shakes
his head, sits down.*) Well — oh Lord! I say — (*He sits in silence,*

shaking his head, gradually stops shaking his head, sits in stillness.) Oh Lord!

Lights.

Curtain.

Methuen's Modern Plays

Jean Anouilh	*Antigone*
	Becket
	The Lark
John Arden	*Serjeant Musgrave's Dance*
	The Workhouse Donkey
	Armstrong's Last Goodnight
John Arden and	*The Business of Good Government*
Margaretta D'Arcy	*The Royal Pardon*
	The Hero Rises Up
	The Island of the Mighty
	Vandaleur's Folly
Wolfgang Bauer,	*Shakespeare the Sadist,*
Rainer Werner	
Fassbinder,	*Bremen Coffee,*
Peter Handke	*My Foot My Tutor,*
Franz Xaver Kroetz	*Stallerhof*
Brendan Behan	*The Quare Fellow*
	The Hostage
	Richard's Cork Leg
Edward Bond	*Saved*
	Narrow Road to the Deep North
	The Pope's Wedding
	Lear
	The Sea
	Bingo
	The Fool and *We Come to the River*
	Theatre Poems and Songs
	The Bundle
	The Woman
	The Worlds with *The Activists Papers*
Bertolt Brecht	*Mother Courage and Her Children*
	The Caucasian Chalk Circle
	The Good Person of Szechwan
	The Life of Galileo
	The Threepenny Opera
	Saint Joan of the Stockyards
	The Resistible Rise of Arturo Ui
	The Mother
	Mr Puntila and His Man Matti
	The Measures Taken and other Lehrstücke
	The Days of the Commune
	The Messingkauf Dialogues
	Man Equals Man and *The Elephant Calf*
	The Rise and Fall of the City of Mahagonny
	and *The Seven Deadly Sins*
	Baal
	A Respectable Wedding and other one-act
	plays
	Drums in the Night
	In the Jungle of Cities